Business Travel Anecdotes

By

Andrew R. Nicoll

Book Layout © 2017 BookDesignTemplates.com[1]

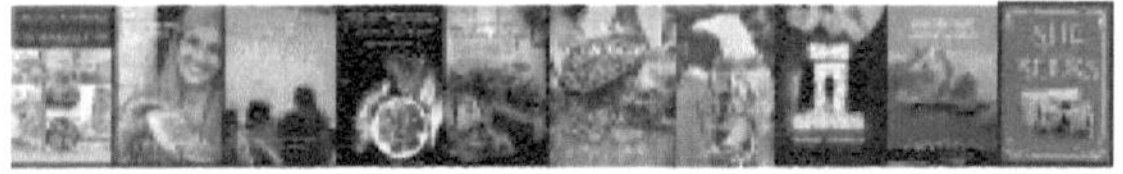

---

1. http://www.bookdesigntemplates.com/

Table of Contents

Dedication

This book is dedicated to my wife Kathryn, who married me over 50 years ago, and my two children, Jonathan, and Stephanie. I was away on business trips for up to three weeks at a time and realize now that nothing can make up for the time lost by being away from the family.

Foreword

Andrew R. Nicoll was born in Exeter, Devon, England in 1949, and studied Metallurgy and Materials Technology at the University of Surrey in Guildford, Surrey. At the time, this was mainly iron and steel. In 1971 he had an opportunity to work for Brown Boveri & Cie in Baden, Switzerland.

He moved to Germany in 1973, doing basic materials research (mainly directional solidification), joining Plasma Technik AG in Switzerland in 1984.

The company discovered that he had a talent for explaining complex technical issues and thus solving customer problems worldwide. He accompanied the global growth of this company and its merger with Metco in 1994, forming Sulzer Metco, a leading player in Surface Engineering.

On 20th February 2009, his position was eliminated because of the "economic crisis". He found sufficient demand as a consultant in Europe, the USA, and Canada to continue until 2019, when he finally retired.

With plenty of time on his hands, he reviewed his travels over the last 25 years. Having kept his boarding cards from over 900 flights, he reconstructed many of his business trips and the incidents that happened along the way. With the photographs and sketches made during many of his trips, this book captures the spirit of the past in a short story form.

Introduction

After school, I attended the University of Surrey in Guildford, studying Metals and Materials Technology for four years. It was a bad year for university leavers. It was September 1971, and I had returned to my parent's home in Exeter, Devon, trying to find a job. The steel industry was down, and 8 of my class 23 had found employment. Devon is the place for tourism, not for technology jobs.

I was in my room at the top of the house when the phone rang.

"Exeter 58450," I said after racing down two flights of stairs and picking up the phone. At the University, the course also included languages (French and German). The language coordinator asked if I would consider filling a German-speaking position at Brown Boveri & Cie (BBC) in Baden, Switzerland, for six months. Not having anything definite in the UK, I said yes. My parents didn't say anything about it, thinking perhaps that I would be back after six months.

On the day of departure, my parents took me to St. David's station in Exeter, and I got on a train to London, followed by a train to Dover. I went to the ferry terminal, bought a one-way ticket to France, and boarded the next ferry. On the French side of the channel, I was met by my girlfriend Kathryn (later my wife) and her parents. We didn't have far to drive as they had a summer house between Calais and Boulogne. Following the weekend, we drove to Paris, and a few days later,

I was on the overnight train to Basel, where I arrived at 6 am. I had some food, took the next train to Baden, and changed some money (£1= 10 CHF). I had the address of the Brown Boveri hostel and managed to find it and check in. I had a room that I shared with a person from Belgium. He seemed to spend all his free time sleeping. Two Egyptians appeared in the washroom separately in the single-story block of rooms. I always wondered why but then discovered they shared a razor blade holder. Each had a separate blade! After a month of living in a shared room, I found a room in Nussbaumen, just across the river from Baden.

To get to work in the mornings, I had to be at the main entrance of BBC in Baden where I got on a bus to take me to the Research Centre. After three weeks, I was called into the HR's office and informed that I was getting a full work and resident's permit. It was September, so the daily temperature at 7.30 was still OK. As we got into October, the temperatures started to drop and I realised that I needed a heavier coat, something I had never experienced in the U.K. In 1972, we started planning for our wedding in Wissant, France. There were numerous documents that had to be translated into French and submitted.

In 1973, my boss announced that he was moving to BBC in Heidelberg, Germany, and more as a joke, I asked him if there was a vacancy for me. We spent 11 years in Germany, where both of our children were born. Toward the end, I was involved with a coating technology (plasma spraying) applying protective coatings to gas turbine blades and vanes. This got to the point where we started an alloy development programme (based on MCrAlY, M= metal, Cr= chromium, Al =

aluminium, Y = yttrium) using additions of tantalum and silicon to increase the operating temperature of the coating. Privately I had contact with the equipment manufacturer (Plasma Technik AG) and started doing translations for them.

My working relationship with my boss fell apart at some point, and I realised it was time to find something else. Luckily, at the same time, the equipment manufacturer, located in Switzerland, was looking for somebody with experience to run the quality laboratory. So, we moved back to Switzerland.

It turned out that the company had decided to expand in the USA and had purchased equipment for a coatings test laboratory. Unfortunately, the idea fell through, so the equipment was shipped to Switzerland, and it was my job to set up the lab in Switzerland. In addition to the lab equipment, we also had a second-hand scanning electron microscope (SEM). Getting the lab up and running, including hiring people, proved interesting. I had inherited a secretary who supposedly could use a typewriter but turned out to be able to run the scanning electron microscope. The second person in the lab came from Oerlikon and during the interview was very nervous. In the end, I asked him what he had in the folder he had brought with him. It turned out that he had examined metallographically all the different steel types that were used at Oerlikon and in all heat-treated conditions. He got the job!

The next project was getting our coating materials approved and specified by Snecma (an aircraft engine manufacturer in France). This involved understanding the powder specifications (in French) and the methods of retesting the materials coming from the USA. We were importing material from a US supplier (Amdry). This project was followed up with getting our equipment qualified at Rolls Royce (RR) in the UK. This was needed to sell equipment to RR engine users (e.g., Saudi Airlines) who were doing their own engine repair and maintenance.

Based on this experience, we now worked on the approvals for General Electric and Pratt & Whitney. At that time, airlines would order the aircraft and engines separately, and there were still four companies (OEM) producing engines; however, today engines are leased based on flying hours, and the OEMs do the repair themselves.

It should be mentioned that we were not alone in the marketplace with the competition coming from the companies Metco and Plasmadyne. However, both companies offered products for plasma spraying but with deficiencies.

The question at the time was:

"How do we cover the expanding market worldwide with our technical advantages?"

Moscow, Minsk
Soviet Union

January 1985

It all started before Christmas 1984 when Mr. Nussbaum, the owner of Plasma Technik, walked into the lab holding a cup of expresso in one hand and in the other one of his favourite Havana cigars. He sat down, sipped his coffee, and asked me to write a report on the company's high-temperature work for a turbine company in the Soviet Union. We had already completed the lab work on the samples we had received, so the report was easy. Having finished the report, I was asked to go to Moscow and Minsk with Erich Brenner in January to present and discuss the report as part of a joint Switzerland-Russia scientific agreement.

I remember that we tried cross-country skiing on 12th January, my wife's birthday. We left for Moscow on Sunday, 13th January, and got on the Aeroflot flight at midday. I recall that we had a baggage security check on the tarmac before we could enter the aircraft and 1st Class comprised 2 solid armchairs side by side behind the cockpit. The outside temperature in Switzerland was minus 13°C.

On arrival in Moscow, we were treated like diplomats and taken through passport control quickly. A woman met us with the driver, as well as a representative from the institute in Minsk. I can no longer recall how the 5 of us, including our bags got into the car. We were driven into the centre of Moscow near the station and had dinner in a hotel restaurant.

Later that evening, we took the overnight sleeper to Minsk. On the train, we ate black bread and drank Vodka; three shots each and the bottle was empty; apparently, this was to celebrate the Russian New Year. Maybe that was just an excuse; who knows? Early the following day, we arrived in Minsk and were met by members of the Institute where the seminar would take place and taken to our hotel.

We got our rooms, showered, changed, had some breakfast, and were taken to the Institute to be shown around and to prepare for our presentations.

View from the hotel in Minsk with a sports arena on the left.

It was a long day, and after dinner in the hotel restaurant, I realised I had been lucky to remember to keep my newspapers from the plane and finish reading them later. I used them to seal up the icy draughts coming through the gaps between the windows and the window frames.

The seminar was planned to comprise three days of presentations and discussions with practical spray demonstrations in the afternoon.

Entrance to the Institute in Minsk

The next day was a shock. The presentation room was packed with probably more than 100 participants from institutes in Moscow and Kyiv. One person had travelled from Vladivostok with a 7-hour time difference.

There was no heating and only single-glazed windows, many of which were broken. The lamp generated the only slight warmth in the slide projector which we had carried with us from Switzerland.

Giving the presentation, I could move around and keep warm, but it was obvious that the translator froze; in fact, many people in the room were turning grey in the face because of the cold.

Giving a presentation with an interpreter has the advantage that you can recap what you have just said while the interpreter is still speaking. On the other hand, the audience was also a distraction as they were suffering from the cold. I was happy to watch a professor taking notes in the front row but then slowly realised that he was using a used envelope which he slowly unfolded to gain maximum space for his notes.

Lunch turned out to be sandwiches in the Institute's professor's office and a 0.5l bottle of cognac which Erich and I happily consumed. At least afterwards, we knew where our feet were located.

From the temperature perspective, the practical sessions with the plasma equipment running turned out to be as cold as the morning sessions. One afternoon session was focused on the technical report I had written about the coatings we had submitted and the tests carried out. A lady technologist or scientist in the audience probably knew as much as I did about the coatings. A very nice discussion started until a political watchdog told her to be quiet and stop asking questions. She wouldn't, so the meeting was closed very quickly, and the people from the institute were sent away, something I had never experienced before. Not exactly freedom of speech or discussion.

Friday night was a relief as the seminar had finished, everybody seemed happy, and we went through the evening ritual of going to dinner with our associates from the institute. On previous evenings we had all had vodka (whether we liked it or not), and typically it was assumed that a good Soviet person would consume at least one bottle himself.

Anyway, the first question came, as always – "What would you like to eat?" which nobody ever seems to answer, followed by "What would you like to drink?" which is always responded to first.

Being a Friday night, I said I would appreciate a glass of wine. I was told that we would have to order a whole bottle of wine, to which I responded that this would not be a problem. Although it was usual to order a bottle of vodka per person, ordering a bottle of wine (for one person) turns you into a social outcast. Anyway, it caused Erich to laugh for a good 5 minutes.

The following evening, we were invited to have dinner with the professor and his wife at his home, and we followed the Soviet tradition of enjoying drinking too much. The differences between the Soviet Union and the rest of Europe could not have been greater. The professor received a few hundred rubles each month but got his 3-room apartment, running costs, car and driver free of charge. His driver took us to the station for the early 8 pm train to Moscow, arriving at 6 am in Moscow with a temperature of 28°C below zero. We were served tea on the train and started a conversation with the carriage concierge, thinking she might be interested in buying blue jeans from us. No way – she wanted vodka, but we didn't have any. We arrived in Moscow at 6 am. We got our luggage onto the platform and proceeded to the exit. Outside to the left, you could see a line of people waiting for taxis.

On the right were taxis arriving with passengers wanting to catch a train. We moved to the right, and with the next taxi, people got out, money exchanged hands, and we got in. The taxi took us to the Hotel Intourist, just around the corner from the National, and we could go to our rooms immediately. We went to bed and then had a late breakfast. We discovered that we had a certain urgency to get some exercise (primarily I suppose to reduce the level of alcohol in the body) and so we walked through the subway to the Red Square, past Lenin's mausoleum, St. Basil's cathedral and then around the Kremlin in the afternoon.

View from the Hotel Intourist in Moscow

Red Square - Lenin's mausoleum on the right, St. Basil's cathedral on the left.

Red Square - Lenin's mausoleum on the left

It was still 28°C below zero as we walked across Red Square, and we were impressed by the number of people waiting to file through Lenin's mausoleum. On the square, we found several one-man stalls selling souvenirs with people huddled around checking things out.

We had begun to wonder where all the people had come from, but by then, we had passed St. Basil's Cathedral, moving down towards the river and seeing all the buses. They had been bused in.

St. Basil's Cathedral from the bus park

Our second week in Moscow was about visiting various ministries to follow up on business opportunities. On one visit, we were informed that we would need to stay an extra day for a specific meeting, and we needed to change our flight tickets. The downside was that it took a whole day to get it done!

I had a morning off as Erich had to go to the ministry, and so I walked to the GUM store on the red square and discovered I was being followed. On one level of the store, I watched how a shipment of Adidas sports clothes was sold out within minutes.

One afternoon in a coffee bar, I made the mistake of taking a sugar cube, dunking it as I would at home, and crushing it between my teeth. Something I had gotten from my mother-in-law in France. Unfortunately, I hadn't realised that the sugar cube would be of a significantly different quality, in this case, very hard, so I cracked a tooth, and two days later, I lost the gold filling.

We had a crab dinner before we left, and very soon, I started running to the bathroom at every opportunity. I was so glad to get on the plane to leave Moscow (with the projector). Unfortunately, the flight was from Moscow to Vienna and then Zurich, and probably due to the Soviet crab, I spent most of the flight in the toilet.

On further trips, I stayed at the National and the Hotel Metropol and had an opportunity to visit the church within the Kremlin walls, where the walls are lined with icons.

The view up to Red Square from the National was the most impressive.

View of the entrance to the Red Square, St. Basil's at the back.

Minsk Soviet Union ..in the Cold

January 1985

We are going on a short outing this afternoon. We haven't been outside the building for a few days, so it will be a nice change. After lunch, we followed our guide downstairs to the car, a Volga, a product of the Soviet Union. It was cold, freezing, but we were well prepared. We climbed into the backseats, and off we went, following the roads out of the city.

View from my taxi

Everything was covered in snow and ice, and we made steady if not slow progress. Outside the city, the road became just a strip of white disappearing into the distance, with very few cars or trucks approaching us.

The heater was trying hard and almost got us to a minimum level of warmth. Occasionally the driver would wind down the window by 3 cm and light up a cigarette, obviously thinking the smoke would leave through the window. He didn't realize that the smoke was coming straight into the back of the car, and it smelt like a bad version of a French Gauloises.

Snow, snow, everywhere

We left the main road, slowly moving along a side road, and finally stopped. To our right was a short wall with an opening and a large sign in Russian, no English. From the car, we could only see the wall but not what was behind it. We got out and moved towards the entrance, wondering what we were doing here and curious to know what the outing was all about. It was cold and we were freezing, especially our faces.

Passing through the opening, an array of fireplaces and chimney stacks extended in front of us, all standing alone. They spread out as far as we could see up to the woods. Woods surrounded the whole place. Standing in the cold, taking in the scene, it slowly became clear that we saw a village's remains. A bell had been placed in every chimney, and they were ringing in different tones and not harmonically. Our guide informed us that each bell in each chimney represented the remains of a family from the village. During the war, the Germans were so fed up with the guerrilla tactics of the locals that they rounded up all the women and children, forced them into their houses, and burnt the houses to the ground. This was a war memorial to the families who had lost their lives.

Memorial

Our faces were so cold that our mouths did not transmit the formulated words. Response had been lost, as well as the ability to explain our emotions.

We returned to the car, lost in our thoughts, trying to cope with the emotions. After a while, we noticed that we were slowly regaining the ability to speak, but the silence remained for quite a while.

Genoa Italy
IIW Meeting

April 1986

The International Institute of Welding (IIW) was that part of the thermal spray community which controlled the decisions on where and how to organize and hold an International Thermal Spray Conference. They were held every three years and, up to this point in time, depended on a local Welding Society for the organization and promotion.

Thermal Spray has little to do with welding. In addition, there were other activities such as writing up, reviewing, and revising ISO documents. The Thermal Spray committee comprised nominated members from different countries, but it was Germany, the UK, Switzerland, France, and the USA who attended the meetings. The chairman was Dr. Malik, from Lufthansa, and meetings were held in different countries. Merle Thorpe and Jack Bender usually represented the USA. Plasma Technik AG hosted one in the Hotel Krone, Lenzburg, Switzerland.

The meeting which I remember most was the one held in Genoa, Italy. The Italian welding society was very keen to have an ITSC conference.

We met at the airport, took taxis to the meeting place, probably a conference room at the hotel, and started our discussions. The meetings were usually held in the afternoon and the following day, allowing easy travel access. In the evening, we walked from the hotel to a small family-run restaurant where we were the only guests.

On the way, we walked past a newspaper stand announcing the Chernobyl disaster. Even though I don't understand Italian, the message was very clear.

The negative news was counteracted by a long-drawn-out Italian dinner with many different courses, literally served by the family running the restaurant.

I slept poorly, wondering why I had been born British and not Italian!

Kyiv Soviet Union

December 1986

We flew to Moscow and changed airports to fly on to Kyiv.

With snow and ice everywhere, we walked out to the plane to Kyiv and, as "privileged passengers", to the steps at the front of the aircraft. Imagining we were on a European flight, we put our bags on the overhead racks and removed overcoats and jackets. However, we didn't know we would sit for 20 minutes with the front, centre, and tail doors open. Watching the other passengers get on, lift the seat, and place their shopping (!) underneath the seat was interesting. Anyway, as it got colder and colder, we decided to put our jackets back on. We finally arrived in Kyiv and left the plane.

The "special" passengers were asked to join the person with the Intourist sign while the rest fought to get on the only bus. After the other passengers had departed, the girl with the sign turned and walked to the arrival building through the snow and ice. I counted 57 planes parked for the night on the way to get our bags in the arrival hall.

People from the Paton Institute met us in the arrival building and drove us to Kyiv. On the way, we passed through sections of the road covered in straw which we were told would help to reduce the spread of fall-out from Chernobyl.

The purpose of the visit was to present what we knew about thermal spray and high-temperature coatings whilst learning about their technologies. Just before lunch on the first day, we were informed that we would be going back to the hotel for lunch. Immediately we thought that we would waste a serious amount of time based on our experience in Minsk and Moscow.

We were led to the restaurant at the hotel and given a table and menus. About five minutes later, we were approached by a rather large waitress who asked simply, "Whadduyuwaant?" in a relatively good American accent. It turned out that over 50 US engineers had spent three months at the Paton learning about oil pipeline welding techniques and had Americanized the hotel. We gave the waitress our order, and it seemed we had our food and drinks, within minutes. It turned out to be a very short lunch every day.

One of the best things that happened in Kyiv was visiting the gold museum. Located on a natural trading route between Siberia and the Mediterranean, the local rulers became seriously wealthy in gold jewellery (rings, brooches, necklaces, headgear, etc), which today is part of a museum.

The other point of interest was visiting the circus - on ice. Everybody knows what to expect at a circus.

Here, of course, everything was different. You must imagine that everything now proceeds on ice with everybody, including the animals, wearing ice skates.

Chimpanzees were buzzing around on ice and, best of all, a cow on skates, actually skating around the circus ring or, in this case a rink.

An interesting evening!

Hongkong Changzhou Shanghai Tokyo

May 1986

I was given seat 21J on a full Swissair flight going to Bombay, Bangkok, and Hongkong. We left on time from Zurich at 1300 and arrived in Hongkong at 9.50 am. the next day. The most fascinating part of the flight to Bombay was flying over the Arabian countries and seeing the natural gas being flared off. It was a 747, and the person next to me at the window was a pilot on his way to Bangkok.

I had been asked to go to a railway factory in Changzhou, about 4 hours by car from Shanghai, and spend a few days talking about coatings using thermal spraying and how they could use our technology in locomotive diesel engines. Arriving in Hongkong, I proceeded to the Meridien Hotel across the bridge from the old airport. The bridge was interesting as it had a conveyor belt for bags. I had a meeting in the afternoon with Bob Clarke at HAECO, an aerospace repair facility located directly at the old airport.

The following morning, I checked out, went back across the bridge into the airport, and checked in for the CAAC flight to Shanghai.

On the flight, we were handed an English version, government questionnaire about AIDS, which nobody understood.

Two people from the Railway Factory met me at the airport with a car and a driver. The driver got us from Shanghai towards Suzhou, Wuxi, and finally Changzhou. We were driven slowly through Shanghai because of pedestrians and then out again towards the VW Shanghai factory. It was the only road sign which I saw on the whole trip. How the driver knew the way is still a mystery. The roads into and out again were full of people on foot or bikes. There were a few other cars and even fewer trucks, but thousands of people seemed to be on the move. We saw a few cars and trucks but basically, it was either people with bicycles or on foot.

Driving away from Shanghai

We stopped for dinner at the Hubin Hotel near Wuxi on the way. My first meal started with perfectly round mushrooms being served as a cold starter and with my low skill level, the mushrooms flew quite nicely. I had been trying to learn to use chopsticks before going on this trip by trying to lift rice grains and transfer them from one plate to another. The Chinese were very amused at my attempts. The food which followed was easier to pick up and eat. We finally arrived at the Baidang Hotel in Changzhou. It had been a long trip from Switzerland, and I was still feeling it.

The railway factory was responsible for repairing and improving large electric locomotives with an R&D Institute that had proposed an improvement program that included purchasing our equipment and materials. This meant that we were interested in ensuring they fully understood thermal spray.

The next day we started with a tour of the Institute's facilities, including powder production using atomization, and a discussion on the seminar's structure. All the basics of surface engineering using Thermal Spraying were split into five sessions with everything being translated as we went. They had already taken the trouble to take our literature and translate and publish it in China.

Lunch was in a restaurant outside the factory compound and was nearly always vegetables with a sauce or thick gravy. In the evenings, there was a dinner for a larger group of people where I was introduced to duck feet and turtle. One afternoon there was an excursion to a large lake near Suzhou which took us through a tea plantation, and we had a flat tyre.

Everybody knows how to change a tyre in most parts of the world. With the low number of cars in China and thus the small number of people being trained to drive, it was only the driver who theoretically knew what to do. I helped him, and the other two Chinese looked on.

Fixing a flat tyre

I was asked if there was anything special I would like to see, and I said I would enjoy being shown around the locomotive factory. The next thing I knew, I was introduced to a short guy in a typical Chinese blue suit and cap. He was the general manager responsible for over 10'000 workers, and he would show me around personally. It was an interesting tour, especially when you recognize how they have gotten around technical difficulties or found alternative ways of doing things rather than importing foreign machines.

The institute had organized a car with a driver to take me back to the airport in Shanghai together with one person from the Institute for translation purposes.

From Shanghai, I flew with Japan Airlines to Narita Airport in Tokyo, which was my first opportunity to try Japanese food. I think I had the noodles. I could take a limousine bus from the airport to the Meridien Hotel Pacific, almost opposite Shinagawa railway station. This was my first visit to Japan, and having got used to masses of people in China, I now had the traffic to deal with as well. During the first night in the hotel, I experienced an earth tremor – like somebody putting their hand on my shoulder and shaking me awake.

The company in Japan had been set up with Marubeni, a large Japanese trading house, and we had an office with a coating development and demonstration area, including our equipment. I got to know the people better and their customer projects during this visit. One day I was asked to go to Kobe to have dinner with people from Tocalo. This company was by far the largest user of Thermal Spray technology, together with other surface engineering methods in Japan. The journey to Osaka, Kobe, and Akashi by train took a long time. I remember that when we finally left the train system and decided to have lunch in a small noodle shop underneath the railway station, it was already nearly 1 pm. We visited the Tocalo plant and then made our way to the Oriental Hotel in Kobe, where in the evening, we met Mr. Nakahira, the president of Tocalo, and Mr. Oka, head of R&D.

Mr. Nakahira, whom I met several times after this trip, gave me a special pocket knife coated with a Tocalo process to make it extra sharp. Unfortunately, many years later, after 9/11 and the increased security measures, it was taken from me during a security check in Washington, even though I had already passed the checks in Frankfurt.

We had Kobe beef together with a bottle of red wine directly out of the refrigerator.

I was glad that I was not paying the bill.

The trip back to Europe with Japan Airlines was uneventful but long with stops in Anchorage, Düsseldorf, and finally Zürich. At least I had plenty of opportunities to shop for souvenirs.

Montreal
Canada

September 1986

"I was wondering if you could take over the organization of our exhibition at the next International Thermal Spray Conference (ITSC)?"

"Well, yes, I suppose I could; where will it be held?"

"In Canada, in fact, in Montreal."

Having bitten off more than I could chew, I now had to get to work. Being at a Thermal Spray Conference with an exhibition, I had a fair idea about what needed to be done regarding marketing messages, new products, and customer benefits. Still, I wasn't too aware of what would hit me.

A booth design, a layout, people to work the booth, customer invitations, exhibitor badges, transportation or equipment for the booth, literature, organizing a product briefing, and so on, but these turned out to be relatively minor compared with working in Montreal.

The booth equipment was on its way from Switzerland to Montreal, and the local booth supplier had our plans and knew when he had exhibition access and when to put up the booth. I had also prepaid part of his contract. Well, the crates arrived in Montreal and were taken to the hall and unloaded onto the ramp. From the ramp, they had to be moved up to the exhibition hall and then in the hall, they needed to be unpacked and cleaned. This involved three different groups, all unionized and working to their local rules which I didn't know anything about.

By the end of the event, including a customer invitation to drinks and snacks I had maxed out 3 credit cards, but I had learned a lot. In addition to the technical exhibition, the conference usually involves technical papers, presentations, and a conference dinner, all of which had to be fitted in somehow.

Plasma Technik AG exhibit in Montreal at the ITSC

Dining with President Nakahira

President Nakahira of Tocalo (Japan) invited me to join him and his wife at their table during the conference dinner, and I discovered that he had an excellent memory, including the dinner we had at the Oriental Hotel in Kobe-Japan during my visit to Japan in early 1986.

Detroit

USA

1986

The message from Mr. Nussbaum was very clear - go to Detroit, visit Alloy Metals, and check it out i.e., is it worth buying, and should he buy it?

My colleague, Dr Eschnauer, a consultant for Plasma Technik was with me. We got reservations with British Airways to London and then through Montreal to Detroit, with somebody from the factory meeting us and taking us to the hotel. On the London to Detroit sector, we had seats on the upper deck of a 747. The only relevant thing which I can recall is that Dr Eschnauer ate lunch twice, and by the time we were due to land in Montreal, he had consumed all of the champagne from the upper galley and had asked for more - to cover the wait in Montreal as we didn't have to leave the plane. It didn't seem to affect him at all.

Alloy Metals was a powder producer using gas atomization technology, making mainly MCrAlY type compositions and other powders for the major manufacturers of aero-engines. We met with their management, reviewed the factory and their work processes, and reported positively to Mr. Nussbaum. Shortly after that, Mr. Nussbaum bought the operation.

Moscow

.. again

1989

Sometimes things develop badly, and you start thinking the worst, but something happens, and everything is all right again.

It was a trip to Moscow to meet customers for a technical discussion about coatings for a paper-making machine. The flight was running late, and finally, we got to Moscow. Usually, I would have changed some money after entering the Soviet Union, but the exchange office was closed because we were late.

I proceeded in a taxi to the hotel, where I checked- in and went to my room to leave my bags and freshen up. No exchange office was available either, so it was a question of going to the restaurant and seeing what happened. On the way in, I spoke to the head waiter, who commented, "No problem, you pay for the food in rubles and the drinks in dollars."

I was led to a table and ordered food and a

bottle of Russian champagne. When it came to paying the bill, the waitress came with the check, and I gave her a US $20 note which was the smallest I had. She looked down at the dollar bill and then back to me, and I noticed that she had started crying. She turned and left, and I got up and left the restaurant. On the way out, the head waiter approached me and explained that, after deducting the check, I had given her more than three months' salary as a tip.

The following day, I was able to change some money, just in case—because after the technical meeting, I was on the plane back to Switzerland.

Kuala Lumpur Malaysia

February 1990

It is true that Malaysians can also sweat. By the time this happens, though, most of us are starting to melt.

It is not yet 6 am, and we are going to the airport. It is hot in Singapore, so we took a taxi. We made our way to the departure building, but before we entered, we followed the building to the right and went through an unmarked door and descended one level, followed by another door.

We found ourselves in a Singaporean food court, literally below the terminal building and even though it was still early, it was pretty packed with people. We found somewhere to sit, look at the different stalls offering food, selected something, and brought it back to the table—shrimp and noodles for breakfast.

What a way to start the day!

After breakfast, we went upstairs and proceeded to the shuttle to Kuala Lumpur—every 30 minutes, just like at the doctor's. You pull a ticket with a number on it and wait until you are called to get on the plane. To make it 30% cheaper, our Singapore agent had not got us ticket reservations, so we had to wait. Luckily, we could get on the next flight as there was no air conditioning in the waiting area.

In Kuala Lumpur, we were supposed to be met by our local agent to visit Malaysian Airlines and the Malaysian Air Force. He didn't turn up, so the next step was to find a taxi and visit Malaysian Airlines. This turned out to be a "get to know you" exercise as all they had was a gigantic hangar, but they had ordered planes with engines from P&W, GEAE, and Rolls-Royce.

We moved on to the Air Force to meet the officer responsible for purchasing, and he suggested that we go for lunch - off-site. Sitting outside under a thatched roof with water running down it for cooling, open on all sides in a nice breeze, we had a delightful lunch. It was hot, and we never got around to business, and even the Air Force officer started to sweat. Apparently, the temperature was over 40°C.

We returned to Singapore the same way as we had come – except that, waiting for the shuttle, we were outside surrounded by concrete walls and little shade and by the time we got on the plane, I was a blob of sweat.

技术讲座

题目：等离子陶瓷涂层的摩擦学性能

主讲人：A. Nicoll. 瑞士PT公司研究发展部主任

时间：1990. 2. 17 上午 9:00—11:30

地点：系馆 4501.

主办：摩擦学实验室

Singapore to Beijing (PRC)

February 1990

Singapore to Beijing with two large suitcases - one full of summer clothing, paper, slides, overheads for presentations I had to give, and a winter bag because Beijing in February can be very cold.

Where do you find a big heavy winter coat in Singapore?

You don't; you bring it with you.

I placed the bags on the weighing machine, and the nice young lady behind the counter proceeded with:

"You are overweight, sir."

I stepped back slowly from the counter and looked down at my winter energy reserves bulging around my waist.

This was followed by apologies. Obviously, she didn't mean me personally.

However, this did bring the supervisor over, but I didn't pay for the overweight bags.

Beijing Shenyang (PRC)

February 1990

I am on my way to Beijing on Singapore Airlines from Singapore. Only about three people were in business class, and the flight attendants became very friendly as we got closer to Beijing Airport. The aeroplanes' approach became exciting, and the first time around, in thick fog, we came down on the left of the runway directly above a herd of sheep. You can probably imagine the second time was more satisfying for the passengers.

Why was I in Beijing? Firstly, to visit our representatives (Bamtri). Secondly, to give a lecture to the Beijing Thermal Spray Society, and thirdly, to lecture at the State Key Laboratory of Tribology, Tsinghua University.

At the first lecture, there were few people, and the room was characterized by having no glass in the windows. This I had learned from lecturing in Minsk. It was cold, with no heating, and snow was falling outside, but I was in my winter clothes, and I kept my duffle coat with me – which I kept on.

The second lecture at the Tribology lab was completely different.

I was introduced to a room full of post-docs, all of whom had studied in the USA and thus not only spoke perfect English but could also ask excellent questions. I survived and was invited to lunch by the head of the lab. I got into his car; the Bamtri people got into their car, and the professor, who had organized everything, got on his bicycle and pedalled through the falling snow to the restaurant.

Sunday turned out to be a free day, and I was offered a private visit to Tiananmen Square and then the Forbidden City, and it was still snowing. We parked on the far side of the square next to the Mao Ze Dong commemorative building and walked across to the main entrance of the Forbidden City.

We must have spent about 3-4 hours going around the Forbidden City. The first thing that hits you is the square's sheer size and the city walls' proportions. One person held an umbrella for me (because it was snowing); another person told me everything I needed to know about the place; another just kept everything under control -politically.

Entrance to the Forbidden City

After this fabulous excursion, I was taken to the airport to make the connection to Shenyang. Unfortunately, the plane had been cancelled because of snow - 2 feet in Shenyang - but nobody had thought of informing the passengers. By chance, I spoke to a Japanese person who was also waiting. Luckily, he also spoke English and discovered that the plane had been cancelled hours before. He was also going to Shenyang.

We decided to return to a hotel somewhere and try the next morning. We took a taxi to the hotel where I had been staying. The hotel sent somebody to the main station and got us tickets on the train to Shenyang the next morning - at 6 am, which meant getting up at about 4.30 am. However, they had to open a new hotel floor just for us - not bad, except that in the first room, I got into bed but couldn't turn off the room lights. This meant changing to a different room. I had ordered breakfast with room service, but of course, it was delivered to the wrong room.

The taxi took us to the main station where we found the track we would have to go to - when the time came. Now I had a briefcase, a bag with overheads and a suitcase and where do people sleep in the main station when they arrive late and depart again early?

You are absolutely correct - on the ground, which means that we had to traverse a collection of bodies with our bags to get to the track where we needed to be.

At 5.45 am, the gates were opened, and we could make our way to the carriage - the soft seat section where we had a very comfortable ride - for about 12 hours. It was foggy for the first couple of hours, and we saw very little. After about 1.5 hours, we were invited to have breakfast in the restaurant car. The restaurant had been cleared of all other passengers, and we were served a three-course meal. An excellent way to help the day along. The same thing happened at lunch, this time a seven-course meal - with beer to drink!

What amazed me most was the food quality and the fact that it was all cooked on an open wood-burning stove in the kitchen.

During the long ride, we were often served tea, which meant that a portion of tea leaves would be put into a large cup, and then it would be filled up to three times with boiling water. After that, the tea leaves would be thrown away, and the procedure started again. The person serving the tea was very proud that she could say, "I cannot speak your language". At least she could say that in English.

Due to the weather and the very flat landscape, the journey up the coast was dreary and dull.

A family got on the train close to Shenyang and joined in on hearing me speaking to a Japanese person in English.

Now, the basic idea was to travel to Shenyang on Sunday, do the training scheme on Monday with our Chinese representatives, and carry out a seminar on Tuesday on thermal spraying. Now I was arriving on Monday evening in Shenyang. The organizers had recognized the problem as the plane had been cancelled and had therefore reversed the program. They carried out the spray demonstration on Monday, leaving Tuesday for me. I also discovered that I did not have any contact information with me; I just knew that I was going to an engine factory that had close ties with GE Aircraft Engines in the USA.

Anyway, the family who had joined us asked if we had a hotel - I didn't, but my Japanese acquaintance did. They were being met at the station, so when we arrived, we were taken to his hotel, which still had a room free for me.

I had been in my room for about 10 minutes when the Japanese person knocked on the door asking me if I wanted to join him and his local agent in the restaurant for dinner. Towards the end of dinner, the conversation turned to me, and I was asked about my plans for Tuesday. I explained what I knew, and the gentleman speaking English and asking the questions left the table, walked over to a wall phone, and telephoned with somebody. He returned to the table and announced that everything was organized for me. We finished dinner and returned to our rooms, and I continued unpacking when the phone rang. When you are travelling and living out of a suitcase, it is a most peculiar feeling to be in a room where nobody can know that you are in that hotel and in that city - and the phone starts ringing. I picked it up.

"Is that Mr. Nicoll?"

"Yes"

"We will pick you up at 8.30 am tomorrow, bye-bye". That was it.

View from my room in Shenyang

I woke up to a dark and misty morning. I had breakfast, and at 8.30 am the following day I was sitting in the hotel foyer waiting for the pick-up, and several large cars pulled up and disgorged a collection of people who all raced towards me.

"Welcome Mr. Nicoll", shake hands ten times, and so on.

We drove to where the seminar would be held, and I prepared my many overheads. After a suitable introduction, I was off into the material using the interpreter. Mind you, the first two rows were full of professors, and the room was long and narrow, so we can only speculate about whether they saw anything sitting at the back.

After about an hour or so, the room suddenly became extremely bright, and I realized that I had two video camera teams approaching me from both sides of the room. It became so bright that nobody could see anything on the screen. Somebody had informed the local TV stations, and I was an instant star for at least 30 seconds.

Anyway, at lunch, I was introduced to the Minister for Science & Technology for that region and many professors, some of whom were entertaining with their English.

On Wednesday morning, we had a wrap-up discussion and exchanged presents. They received a picture book of the mountains from Switzerland, and I was presented with a video of my presentation. In the afternoon, I was taken to the "original" Forbidden City which is in Shenyang. I was told that what I was seeing had been used as the model for what was built in Beijing – just 20 times larger. It was here that I suddenly found myself alone and surrounded by Chinese. My guys had gone to find some soft drinks, and the Chinese group was getting closer and closer. I couldn't think about what I should do, and then a woman stepped forward and ran her finger down the side of my face. Luckily, the drinks arrived at that moment, and it was explained to me that the Chinese group had never seen a white person before.

In the evening, I met up with the Japanese person again, and we went for dinner and then to a dance bar where it seemed normal for the men to dance together and the women to do likewise.

Otherwise, the beer was very acceptable.

HONG KONG

Shenyang Shanghai Hongkong Frankfurt Zurich

February 1990

A car had been arranged to take me to the airport for my flight to Shanghai from Shenyang. With my entourage leading the way, we stormed to the front, and I was checked in. The check-in desk was a scrum with people fighting to get to the head of the line. We said our goodbyes, and I was left to wait. Looking out of the departure lounge window, I could see a few Chinese-built DC9s planes, parked a long way away.

As I expected we were shown to an open door, our boarding cards checked and then we marched across to the plane. I was dressed in my winter outfit, which included a heavy duffel coat. I was very well insulated, but the other passengers did seem to be dressed very lightly for the cold wind and slight snow dusting on the tarmac.

When it came to getting on board, people were already on the steps complaining that they weren't allowed on. As I came into view, the flight attendants standing at the door started to send everybody down and let me come up first, something I found embarrassing. I had seat 1A, and there was a Japanese person in 1B. We started a conversation in English and almost kept it up until we got to Shanghai. I think he liked the idea of the opportunity to practice. A food box and orange juice were served during the flight. Interestingly, one of the passengers came forward with a music cassette, and the flight attendant put it into a player and played it.

We arrived in Shanghai, got on a bus, and were taken to a corner of the airport where a carousel seemed to be standing on the edge of a field. There was a wooden hut behind it where passports were checked.

C. T. Tan from our Singapore office had agreed to meet me at airport arrivals, so I stood in my duffel coat with two suitcases and a briefcase. Nothing happened for 40 minutes, and then suddenly, a taxi stopped in front of me, and the Japanese person from the plane asked me if I wanted to ride with him to his hotel and then take the taxi to my hotel. I had transportation but didn't know which hotel C. T. Tan had reserved for us.

As with all visits to new cities, you go through a quick review – Marriott, Westin, or Hilton?

I selected the Hilton, and that's where the taxi took me.

I was given a room on the 31st floor and was met by a Hilton VP with a large basket of fruit on the way to my room. There was an impressive line of porters standing in a line outside the hotel, so my bags disappeared quickly. The front desk was more than a little surprised to have somebody turn up without a reservation. However, shortly after the Tiananmen square issues and many cancellations, they were pleased to see me.

These were the days of landlines, not mobile telephones, and the question was, "Where is C.T. Tan?"

I called his office number in Singapore, but nobody knew where he was. I called his private number, and his wife told me that he was meeting Mr. Nicoll at Shanghai airport.

Anyway, things were not so bad. I had a hotel room, a fantastic view of the building activities around the hotel, a public park with people exercising, and a basket of fruit! The telephone rang. "Could I speak to Mr. Nicoll, please?" It was C.T. Tan calling from the airport. He had gone to the airport early and had been told that the plane was delayed because of snow in Shenyang. He had gone away and had some lunch and then returned and asked again about the plane from Shenyang. This time he was told that the plane had arrived an hour ago, and everybody was gone. He asked if there was a large European in a heavy winter coat with several bags. "Yes, he got into a taxi with a Japanese person."

At this point, CT went through the same iteration that I had gone through - Marriott, Westin, or Hilton? After a few calls, he found me at the Hilton.

Shanghai – can you count the number of buses?

We visited the Institute of Ceramics at the University during our stay in Shanghai. They had received a gift of a piece of our equipment from MIT in the USA, which wouldn't function. A wire had come loose. They feared taking a screwdriver to it, so I did it for them.

We also visited a company in Wuxi and paid a courtesy visit to the Railway Factory in Changzhou.

The day arrived, and I had to fly back to Europe. CT had left in the morning back to Singapore. I had a car arranged to take me to the airport, and we arrived with plenty of time, although the road was still almost only a single file. The driver took my bags, and suddenly a tall person in a long winter coat grabbed both bags and started marching towards the airport building with me trying to keep up. He must have been about the tallest Chinese person I have ever seen. Seen from the back I had no idea who or what he represented. He was heading towards a large door marked arrivals and ploughed through the people standing around. I was still right behind him. It slowly dawned on me that in the arrival hall, departures were on one side and arrivals on the other, and he was heading directly for the Departures desk. My arrival from Shenyang had been outside in the field!

He got to the counter, put down my bags, and turned around. He had Hilton across the front of the coat. He had seen the Hilton labels on my bags and just grabbed them, thinking he could help without trying to speak any English.

He was happy, and I was pleased.

I checked in through Hongkong, Frankfurt, and Zurich. The Cathy Pacific flight to Hongkong was 2 hours late, and the departure lounge suffered from a lack of glass in the windows and almost no heating. We finally boarded, and I found myself next to one of the most beautiful Chinese girls I had ever seen, but unfortunately, she did not speak English.

It got worse. To enter Hongkong, she had to fill out an immigration form, and it became apparent that she could not read or write. She had to ask a flight attendant to help her.

The pilot tried hard, but we still arrived with a 2-hour delay in Hongkong. The plane, a brand new 747-400, had come in from Australia with many transit passengers, and the back door was jammed shut so all economy passengers had to go through business to get to their seats. The transit desk was a mess, and I ended up with a handwritten boarding card. The lifts were not working, so I had to walk and eventually found the gate for the flight to Frankfurt. I showed them my boarding card and took the brunt of frustrated ground personnel having a tough day.

But enough is enough, and when I finally opened my mouth and requested the gate manager, they discovered that I was speaking English compared to Hongkong-English. Having ensured I had a seat on the plane, I retreated to a far corner and waited for boarding to start. However, when boarding for economy finally started, the gate personnel thought it would be good to ask me to go on first – in front of all the tired and frustrated economy transit passengers. I refused. It was a long flight to Frankfurt, about 14 hours. At night they opened the galley with sandwiches and drinks for people to serve themselves. Quite a nice idea!

We arrived in Frankfurt, and the plane emptied almost completely. As I was in transit, I stayed where I was, which in those days was typical. I was comfortable, and I did not want to have to move. Somebody from the Cathy Pacific ground staff in Frankfurt started to move through the cabin and asked me for my boarding pass upon seeing me. She looked at it, recognized it was handwritten, and immediately accused me of sneaking on board in Frankfurt to fly to Zurich. With everything that had happened so far, I had to control myself. I asked for the gate manager, who finally appeared, complaining that he had more important things to do at the gate. He looked at the boarding card, spoke aggressively to the woman, apologized, and disappeared. I have never flown with Cathy Pacific since.

技术讲座

题目：等离子陶瓷涂层的摩擦学性能

主讲人：A. Nicoll 瑞士PT公司研究发展部主任

时间：1990. 2. 17 上午 9:00—11:30

地点：系馆 4501.

主办：摩擦学实验室

Wuxi (PRC)

February 1990

I arrived in Shanghai from Shenyang by plane, and we are going to a textile factory in Wuxi on the train from Shanghai. It is cold, and the heating is just a stove at the end of the railway carriage, fed with lumps of coal when needed and connected to some water circulating system. I have my winter stuff with me. CT Tan had his Chinese woollen gear underneath his suit. A problem with a piece of spray equipment needs to be dealt with. If we don't deal with the problem, we could negatively influence further sales through a ministry in Beijing.

Our discussions proceeded very cautiously, the intention being that we would add amendments to the original contract. In our sales discussions, we relied on the customer's translation of his equipment specification. Now at the factory, we discovered that the customer had not translated the specification correctly into English. So now we are faced with positively influencing future sales and making sure that the customer doesn't lose face.

We were staying in a local hotel, but my room consisted of a conference room for 20 people, a bedroom, and a bathroom. On the day we wanted to finalize the amendments to the contract, the people from the factory realized that they had no electricity in their factory. They only had electricity on six days of the week - so I invited them to my hotel "conference room" to finalize our discussions and the contract amendments.

Everything went very well, with all points being cleared up and put into writing. We even managed to organize having

them served tea during the discussions. Afterwards, we wondered if they had ever been in a Western-style hotel before and that they were more impressed by the hotel rather than by our "fantastic" arguments.

Barcelona, Gijon, Madrid
Lisbon

November 1990

Jordi Garcia was originally our salesperson for Spain and Portugal and, during a visit to the plant in Switzerland, suggested that we should organize a tour of his area, giving technical presentations. We met at the airport in Barcelona and drove into town for some lunch, followed by a presentation at the University. They were interested in opening a department for surface engineering.

The following day, we were at the airport early for the shuttle to Madrid. We were checked in, our bags were gone, and we were in the departure area when we realized that the shuttles weren't flying at all – fog in Madrid. Everything had been cancelled, so the next thing to do before leaving the airport was to rearrange our flights. We got a reservation for a flight to Gijon, which was on our itinerary anyway.

We decided to spend the day visiting Barcelona, especially the area where Jordi had spent his college days working in the old part of the city, enjoying a wonderful paella in a restaurant right next to the water.

We took a plane to Gijon and got picked up by a customer who took us to dinner at 10 pm—a seafood restaurant with steel tables and chairs and lots of sawdust on the floor. I soon realized the procedure, just like in Singapore in a seafront restaurant. You attacked the shrimp, crab, and lobster with your hands, and the bits of the shell got dropped on the floor.

Desert turned out to be a blue cheese dish mashed up with calvados at the table.

The following day was reserved for a presentation at the local Polytechnic, and then in the afternoon, it was back to Madrid, allowing us to fly on to Lisbon the next day. We saw the inside of a lot of airports.

In Lisbon, we stayed in a hotel that reminded me very strongly of the communist style, as seen in Moscow or even East Germany. As before, it was a case of giving a presentation at the University on "Coatings using Thermal Spray", emphasizing the superiority of the coating process.

The following day at the airport, we split. Jordi went back to Barcelona, and I was going back to Zurich, at least that's what I thought!

We were in fog when the pilot said we were landing. I even asked at the TAP check-in desk why flying to Zurich would take so long. We were in Geneva, and after 45 minutes, we started again for Zurich.

As they always said, TAP means "Take Another Plane"!

Note: Over the next two years, Jordi followed up each presentation by selling a coating system to each University and Polytechnic, respectively.

Seoul to Taipei

February 1992

I was on my way to Taiwan with Bob Clarke. We would repeat a seminar on what we had done in Seoul with several customer visits.

It takes at least three hours if not more than you think. Two white, European faces on an Airbus 300-600 sitting in row 55 or was it 66. Who cares? It was a long aircraft with one class. We had been in Seoul to give a seminar on thermal spraying, and now we were on our way to Taipei to repeat the exercise. It was the start of a long vacation in Korea, and the plane was more than full.

They started the meal service, and it took ages to get to where we were sitting. We noticed several rows in front of us that the flight attendant pushing the cart kept pulling up a card and mouthing something. When he got to us, he turned and said, "Would you like the meat or the fish?"

We both replied that we would like the meat and going back to his card, he said,

"I am sorry, sir; I only have the fish."

OK, so we got the fish, not a big deal, but with nothing to go with it. They finished moving through with their carts and returned to the galley at the front of the plane. A few minutes later, the same flight attendant appeared, walking up the aisle towards us with a bottle of red and white wine in his hands.

"Sir, would you like some wine?"

"Yes, I said and took the white wine bottle from him."

Bob doesn't enjoy alcohol, so the guy was left standing in the aisle with a bottle of red wine and no card with his English written out for him.

He returned to the front, and I enjoyed the white wine.

In Taipei, we met with our representative at the airport and drove to Hsinchu. We visited Taipei, Hsinchu, and Taichung where we visited the local university for our seminar. We didn't get around to any sightseeing and we seemed to be constantly travelling in the dark.

Staying in Hsinchu was interesting, and the views of the city during the day and in the early evening turned out to be quite fascinating. One evening after dinner, we decided to stroll directly outside the hotel. It was all lit up, but parked scooters almost completely blocked the sidewalks. We finally crossed the street and moved into a night market, selling almost everything. It had plenty of side alleys and of course, we got lost. Eventually, we found our way out and back to the hotel. The following morning all the scooters were gone.

Arriving at the airport in Taipei for our flight to Singapore, I overheard the two people in front of us saying that they were checking in to fly to Singapore and then on to Zurich for a vacation. I asked them politely if they knew the weather in Switzerland as it was already freezing, and they would need an overcoat or a winter jacket. They became immediately concerned but decided they would have to buy something on arrival.

Except, it is challenging to buy a winter coat on arrival before leaving the airport.

Singapore

February 1992

Bob Clarke and I were staying at a hotel just off the end of Orchard Road. It wasn't a bad place, except that CT Tan, our representative in Singapore, had made the reservations for us, the seminar, the lunch, etc., so everything was priced accordingly. We met in the hotel and agreed to go through our presentation material again before the seminar started. In those days, we had plastic overheads which, in the case of a daylong seminar, you had quite a few, and they weighed a ton. So, we met up in one of our rooms and started sifting through our overheads, spreading things as we proceeded.

We got to the point where we decided that we needed some coffee and asked room service to send up some coffee.

"How much coffee do you need, sir?"

"Oh, well, I think about three cups each. Yes, that would be nice, and there are two of us".

European logic would say that you have three cups for each of the two people, which means six cups of coffee (in a flask to keep it hot), served on a tray with two cups and saucers, and pour it when it arrives.

It didn't take too long, and the doorbell rang, and in came room service amid all of our overheads and papers for the seminar. The tray was put down, we signed the receipt and room service left.

It was then that we noticed that we had a tray with 6 cups and saucers, all full with coffee, and a full flask of hot coffee.

So much for European logic!

After our preparation, we took a taxi along the beachfront until we came across a food/activity centre, where we hired two mountain bikes and pedalled around for some time. My bike had a full set of gears but only one would work, and Bob's bike didn't have any brakes.

The weather was nice, though!

Aachen Germany

Underwater Plasma Spraying (UPS)

July 1992

The founder and owner of Plasma Technik AG, Mr. Nussbaum, asked me to join him and his wife for dinner in the Movenpick Hotel near Zurich to meet Professor Erich Lugscheider from Aachen University in Germany. The food was good, and the conversation very general, but the ideas started flowing as soon as the meal ended. Erich Lugscheider believed that running plasma spray equipment underwater must be possible. He had a water tank in his institute. He had students – he just needed some equipment. Mr. Nussbaum listened, lit up one of his cigars, and said yes, Erich Lugscheider had his full support, and I would be the person to coordinate everything.

As time progressed, there were regular visits to Aachen to see how things were progressing and eventually a technical paper was written and presented at the ICMC, a conference held every year in San Diego, USA. I was present at the conference in my role as a program director for thermal spraying and during the conference dinner Erich Lugscheider was presented with the best paper award at the conference. Christine, Erich Lugscheiders wife, was with him at the dinner. We had to pass the swimming pool on the way back to our hotel rooms. She asked me to hold her bag for a minute and dived head-first into the pool. Quite a character!

View from the hotel in Aachen.

Most of our industrial customers responded to the idea of UPS almost negatively, except for GE Nuclear in San Jose.

I had been back in Switzerland for over a week when the phone rang, and an American wanted to speak to me from California. It was a Thursday afternoon.

"Could I come and see you and look around Plasma Technik and then visit Aachen with you?"

I agreed straight away, and we got everything organized. Henry Offer from GE visited Switzerland, toured the plant and the Institute in Aachen, saw the experimental equipment running, and then returned home. He called again two weeks later to say he had his project financing and would start experimental work in Aachen shortly. In total, he carried out more than 1400 tests underwater.

His financial controller decided to come over as well, so I met him at Cologne airport and we drove to Aachen, followed by a visit to the plant in Wohlen, Switzerland.

In the end, GE Nuclear purchased several pieces of equipment which were used on 1st generation nuclear power plants in Japan to replace metal that had been lost due to corrosion.

Years later I had the opportunity to visit Henry in San Jose. He still had his equipment for experiments but basically funding for this area had dried up completely.

Seoul
South Korea

1992

I had instructions about the limo bus from the airport to the Intercontinental hotel. I had made it to Seoul, and the weather was good. I changed some money, found the ticket office, bought a ticket, and found the bus. Even though I was pretty tired from 10 hours of flying time in a Korean Air 747SP, I was fascinated by the scenery and the plastic-covered fields where the white cabbage for the Kimchi is grown. And I was going to find out that it is served with nearly every meal. The 747SP must have been one of the original ones - little overhead space and seats tight together with little legroom. The one I arrived in had started in Rome and was full when it arrived in Zurich.

Arriving at the bus station, it was a very short walk to the hotel. Standing in the line to check in, a voice said, "Welcome to Seoul Mr. Nicoll". Next to me was the concierge asking me to accompany her to a different desk where everything was already waiting for me.

How did they know? I never found out, even though it happened on all subsequent visits to Korea.

I felt exhausted on the evening of my arrival due to the time lag and insufficient legroom on the plane. After a shower and testing the bed (nice and soft), I headed downstairs for some food. It was a "western style" buffet, so I could select things without being exposed to Korean food and getting into trouble.

Returning to my room, I noticed a narrow high door next to the window on the left, almost covered by a side curtain. I discovered a smoke mask and a knotted rope, long enough to throw it out of the window and climb down should the hotel catch fire, but it seemed only from the 8th floor. So, what did you do if you were on the 9th floor or above? I was prepared for everything – but in the meantime, I was so tired that I just went to sleep.

Trips in Korea were always short – within Seoul or to Pohang, Ulsan, Daejeon, Changwon-City, and Taejeon, either flying or in the car. Flights are all less than one hour on basically a shuttle service. In all cases, it was a visit intended to demonstrate our technical activities and products. Landing in Pohang, the first thing which hit me were the anti-aircraft gun installations along the side of the runway. Interesting! We visited the steel R&D centre (Pohang Steel is one of the major players worldwide). We saw steel rolls for an annealing plant being sprayed with chromium carbide – nickel chrome material using our equipment. The coating had been developed by Tocalo in Japan and licensed to Pohang. Leaving the plant in a taxi, we had to cross a railway line, and the driver didn't see a train approaching rather quickly. We almost got wiped out by a liquid steel transporter. In Changwon City we visited Samsung, and I was held to be a spy as I had a camera with me (which I had declared on entering the plant). The discussion became very heated between the security guards and my associates from Korea. Luckily, I couldn't understand what was being said.

After many visits to Korea, the one day off was after a thermal spray seminar with Bob Clarke in Seoul. Unfortunately, the seminar was not really all that successful. The literature from our powder manufacturing site in Troy, Michigan, covering our spray powders and brazes products failed to arrive in time.

However, we managed to go sightseeing and went to the top of the hill overlooking the city, a shrine followed by a visit to the leather market where you could only buy in US dollars. Bob still thought it would be cheaper in Hong Kong.

The next stop was Taipei.

Orlando

USA

The Green Tube to Orlando

May 1992

There was a time when there was a need to visit General Electric in Cincinnati regularly. This involved a flight to Chicago followed by a connection to Cincinnati. Luckily, we had a salesperson based there to look after General Electric, so I had local transportation. On one occasion, a trip was combined with participation in a conference and exhibition in Orlando. Instead of flying, the suggestion was to drive down Interstate 75 to Orlando. Having only seen the US from the air, this sounded very interesting.

We left at 6 am on a Saturday and headed south on the highway into Kentucky and on towards Atlanta. As we progressed, the highway split into two parts, and the trees got taller, denser, and edged closer until we were driving down a green tube. It seemed to me that I just kept falling asleep until we stopped again to gas up the car. We kept going, and just before Atlanta, the trees started to move back and released us back into civilization. After Atlanta, it began to become flat and get dark late in the afternoon.

We arrived in Orlando at about 12.30 at night, and I had only seen the inside of a green tube.

Moscow/Minsk

Soviet Union

March 1992

We were on our way to Minsk again.

For 3000 Francs in Swiss currency, we were financially supporting a Plasma Technik seminar at the Institute in Minsk. Not necessarily legally correct, but interesting. The seminar went better than expected with a lot of participants. My colleague was the one carrying the money.

We discovered that a "dinner" had been organized for the seminar participants, and we were the main guests sitting at the head table, with myself on the left of the President of the Institute.

Soon everybody was seated, and the dinner got underway. Before anything was served, I was feeling thirsty and seeing two bottles of mineral water in front of me, I took hold of a bottle, opened it, and poured myself some water. I picked up the glass and was just about to drink when the large left hand of their president descended onto my right arm and stopped me from moving it any further.

"Mr. Nicoll, that is vodka, be careful."

I looked again at the label on the bottle. The bottle was a water bottle, and the label was a typical water bottle label. Ingenious, and with two bottles for everybody present. By now, I thought everybody from the institute had been invited to join us for dinner.

The dinner proceeded, and after the first course, the president stood up and gave his little speech with somebody doing the interpreting for us, followed by everybody draining their water (vodka) glasses. The glasses were quickly refilled. No lack of lubrication here. The second course was served, and I realized then that it would be my turn to say something. The nice thing about an interpreter is that you have time in between to think about what comes next, especially if you have never done this kind of thing before. So I got up and got on with it, raising my glass at the end.

And so, it proceeded between the president and me for quite a few courses. Somehow my colleague - the money carrier, didn't get involved. From somewhere, music started, and dancing commenced. By then, everybody had consumed a massive amount of vodka; each person had had two bottles on the table before them! The result was that they couldn't stand anymore, let alone dance.

The next time I will carry the money i.e., no speeches!

South Korea

The Presidents Suite - 1992

We visited Samsung in the south of Korea. We arrived at the Samsung main factory entrance and went through the usual procedure of being asked questions: "Do you have a camera with you?" – "Yes, I do", being directed to a building, giving a presentation, listening to technical questions, all of this through an interpreter, being thanked for coming, and then leaving again. The first thing that hit me was how short the people were as we exited the airport arrival building.

However, we left by a different gate.

The guys at the gate had a field day as they searched my bag and discovered – the camera. Despite all attempts of diplomacy, they had found a camera, and I was the wicked white face. We got them to accept, at least, that we could return with an escort to the main gate.

The problem disappeared, I got my camera back, and we left.

As we were staying overnight, we headed into town and found our hotel. As was usual in Korea, I got the Westerners' room, and the Koreans did whatever they did. Except, for whatever reason, I had the President's Suite, which occupied the whole top floor of the hotel. It wasn't very comforting having so much space! The bathroom had all the usual things in it and, in addition, a sauna. It had a bath mounted at the top of 3 marble steps. It looked so good that I decided the sauna, followed by a soak, would be a good idea. After my bath, I stood up in the bath, put one foot on the top marble step, which by now was wet, and had to think twice about how I would get down the steps. I made it but didn't take a second bath.

Located on one half of the top floor, I had two lounges and huge television sets with seating for about 10 in each one, a maid's room, a bathroom with an elevated marble bath, a shower, and a sauna, admittedly only big enough for two people. There were two giant size bedrooms and a full-size conference room with seating for approximately 20 people.

It was scary. Coming back from dinner I started out by putting on all the lights, closing the curtains, and making sure I was alone.

I was, and considering everything, I slept quite well.

India

January 1993

The day started badly. It was a Friday. My colleague and I arrived at the Swissair terminal to check in for the 12 o'clock flight to Bombay, but I was told that it wasn't possible for them to check me in as I didn't have a visa. The fact was that I hadn't been told about it.

My colleague checked in and took my bag with him; Swissair rearranged my flight via London and then to Bombay, and I was left with an afternoon to take the train to Bern, visit the Indian Embassy, and get my visa.

This was the middle of January, and I had arrived at the airport with just a sweater. We were going to India, where it would be hot. I took the train to Bern, had some photos made in a machine at the station, and took a taxi to the embassy. For a change, the sun was out, and it was a relatively warm day for January.

Luckily, I had a letter of invitation with me from India, so the paperwork was duly completed. I was told that it would cost 80 Francs and that I had to pay at the local post office, which I did, and after that, I was given my passport back with the visa stamp. All I needed to do now was return to the main station, but I had no cash left for a taxi, so I walked it. I eventually reached the station, took the train to Zurich airport, and got on a BA flight to London. We circled above London for 30 minutes before we could land, and afterwards, I still had plenty of time. I found the terminal and gate for Bombay departing at 11 pm and sat at a bar watching the gate until the flight was called. This was fascinating, as even before the flight was called, masses of Indians started to crowd around the entrance, like a giant scrum, like a rugby match. Still, with far more people, everybody pushing, the families trying to keep together, to say nothing about the huge number of bags they were taking on board. Boarding finally started and the mass of passengers maintained its momentum until finally, it was time for me to join the end of the queue and get on board.

It was interesting to see that the concept of seat numbers was unknown to many. Families just sat down together. I had a seat in the economy just behind a bulkhead, so I had plenty of room to stretch. Apart from a tropical storm during the flight, it was uneventful.

The flight arrived around 8 am in Bombay and with just my hand luggage it was very easy for me to get through immigration, customs and change some money. I had arranged with my colleague, Dieter Schmid, that we would meet at the airport, and there he was. He arrived at midnight, found the hotel (Centaur Juhu Beach) and returned to the airport for my arrival. We decided on a taxi, got in, and it wouldn't start. We got out and pushed with the driver in the car until it jump-started.

Getting to the hotel and checking in was uneventful. We were due to visit existing and potential customers giving presentations and while travelling all over India. We met up with our representatives from CUMI in Madras for a short discussion on our programme in India. Ravi and Kamban both spoke excellent English.

The hotel backed onto a beach, and after some lunch, we decided to take a short walk down to the water. On the beach, we were approached by a woman begging. She was holding a small girl in her arms, but the girl only had one hand. It was afterwards that we learned about the "official" going rate for beggars (at the time, it was 60 Indian cents) and what people do to increase their chances of getting money. We returned to the hotel and had our first introduction to vegetarian Indian food that evening in the hotel restaurant – "Not too spicy, please".

On Sunday, we decided that we had better see something of the city and went to the visitor's desk in the hotel. We took a car with a driver for the day. 1000 Rs turned out to be the equivalent of 20 CHF. The driver took us around all the major sites, including the Gateway of India and Victoria Station. Our driver recommended that we visit Elephanta Island, which involved getting on a ferry and about a 20-minute trip. Military observers on the ferry stopped people from taking pictures of the military installations and warships in the harbour.

Gateway of India

Victoria Terminus Railway Station

Elephanta Island

The Elephanta Island is a large piece of granite into which a truly spectacular temple has been carved. On leaving the ferry, we were first told to avoid the monkeys as they bite – charming. Our experience with begging had put us in the position of knowing the going rate, and we were armed with 60 cents for each one who asked.

The American tourists didn't know the situation and started giving the beggars rupees and dollars. At least it kept them away from us. At the time, the existence level in India was 4 rupees a day. So, a few hours of begging with tourists who didn't understand the going rate or the Indian social system turned out to be quite lucrative for the beggars.

The week before we arrived in Bombay, there had been tremendous racial strife, with over 1600 people being killed.

We had expected Ravi and Kamban to join us, but they had also heard about the racial strife and called off. We became very aware of this as we returned to our car. The driver was agitated and insisted that we drive as quickly as possible back to the hotel. On the way, he avoided those areas of the city where he felt he might be attacked. We were treated to our first exposure to large cockroaches in the hotel lift going up to our floor. Again, something you must get used to.

On Monday morning, it was back to business and a visit to Air India. On the way the car broke down and we arrived late. We were also stunned by the traffic, mainly double-decker buses, three-wheelers and high emissions.

At Air India, we had a tour of their workshops and recognized a few aerospace parts which other customers were also reconditioning. The visit concluded with a meeting with the Superintendent who sat behind a very large wooden teak desk and asked:

"Why is your equipment so expensive compared to the competition"?

Traffic on the roads of India

"We save you money", was my reply, and the conversation moved on with an in-depth description of why our equipment is better. Luckily on our plant tour, we saw a GE engine component that we knew Haeco in Hongkong was coating in 4 hours. This surprised the superintendent as the same part with their installed equipment took nearly two weeks.

After lunch, we gave several presentations to the technical people at Air India. We returned to the hotel to get our bags and were caught in heavy traffic. We were taking a train north to Vadodara (Baroda) that evening, but because of the racial strife, we had to be at the station as early as possible. We arrived at 7.50 pm, and we were locked into the train. The curfew started at 9 pm, and the train wasn't leaving until 11.20 pm. To find our sleeping berths, we had to search for a list stuck on the outside wall of the carriage. We were in a 6-berth AC sleeper.

We checked into the hotel (Surya Palace) the following day, just after 6 am. We had reservations for early check-in, but things went wrong. The rooms weren't ready for Ravi and Kamban, and my room had no towels, so a shower was out of the question. The view from the window was interesting, looking out into a yard with two cows.

Cows get everywhere.

I decided to go for a short walk – to the local post office to send a few postcards. There were more cows in the streets, but that was about all. I found the post office, and I entered—with the front door open. It was dark. As my eyes got used to the darkness, I recognised that about ten men were sitting in a circle on the floor sorting the mail with letters flying in all directions. I suppose that each person is responsible for a particular area or street. I was told to come back later – when they were open!

Back in the hotel, we met for breakfast and then visited a fertilizer plant which proved to be a mistake, but they did take us to lunch for having come so far. After returning to the hotel, we discovered that there was a Maharaja's palace in the town, which turned out to be closed to the public, but there was also a small museum with lots of Asian exhibits. After dinner, we met to discuss our company event being held in the hotel on the next day. Afterwards, we went down for a beer and at the bar were suddenly invited to go down into the lower-level reception area where an Indian wedding was taking place as "special guests" we were taken up onto the stage and introduced to the bride and groom.

By the time I got back to my room, I had towels, but I also came across a collection of candles and matches. At 11.15 pm the lights in the hotel failed!

The following day I was able to shower, well that was until I discovered a major leak in the bathroom. The company event started at 10 am and finished at 5 pm with everybody giving presentations. Unfortunately, we only had 20 people attend due to train delay, and an air strike etc. We were invited to a mini-bus tour of the town visiting a temple (no shoes), we checked out, collected our bags from the hotel, told the manager what we thought and went to the station arriving at 8.15 pm for a train at 9.25 pm to Delhi. We finally left at 10.30 pm.

It was fascinating on the platforms to watch the people at the food stalls both cooking and eating. Small groups would gather around a one-man stall, eat something, and then move on to the next.

Food stall

Small savoury pies (above) or fried chilli peppers, the small ones wrapped in newspaper, seemed to be the favourite.

By now, we had realised how our agent had organised our visits – take the train overnight, check in, have lunch and do a company visit. On the train, we were served dinner where we were sitting, and the next morning, we got breakfast as well. This time I was in the left upper bunk, 1st class AC sleeper, but I was directly under the air vent, which let out the cold air. The two people in the lower bunks were still chatting at 12 pm, so I had to ask them to be quiet. Around 9 am, it slowly became light enough to take photographs. The windows were filthy, but as we travelled through the outskirts of Delhi, there were lots of interesting scenes of village life right up beside the railway line.

We finally arrived at 10 am and arrived at the Shervani Fort View Hotel at 11 am. Thin walls and draughty! We had an appointment with Air India and finally left the hotel at 12.30. We met the Engineering manager and went through the repair shop. Afterwards, we visited a company making printing presses. On the way back to the hotel we stopped at the Centaur Hotel for "a snack" as we hadn't had any lunch and then went looking for a scarf as it was very cool outside.

Now buying a scarf is more complicated than you think because in India you have to get the length correct. You wrap it around your head vertically and then around your neck and tuck it in. Now you have the correct length and can choose the material and colour. I chose a light brown mohair scarf which I finally lost going through La Guardia airport in New York several years later.

In Delhi, we had one main visit to BHEL in the afternoon and so the morning was filled with sightseeing, in particular Connaught Place, the ceremonial avenue of the Republic, the Red Fort and Qutb.

Strolling across Delhi

India Gate

Ancient buildings and monuments

Monuments, Qutab Minar

Driving in Delhi proved to be more frightening than in Bombay. We were on a road with three lanes in each direction, and we were driving on the left. Now imagine that your driver wants to overtake, and he is doing this in the fifth lane from the left, and traffic keeps coming towards you!

Travelling by taxi in Delhi

Our next stop was Calcutta, and we needed to get to the airport early as we had been told that we only had standby seats. As usual, there was a problem – we needed to check out of the hotel fast, but it didn't happen. After 20 minutes, the manager arrived, and we managed to pay and leave. It was afterwards that I was told the person at the front desk dealing with us could not read or write.

It would help if you were prepared for everything. We flew to Calcutta, arriving in the dark at 9 pm and took a bus into the city. Yes, the driver would take us directly to our hotel. It was dark, and the bus had no glass in the windows, but at least the airflow kept us cool.

The driver got lost, but eventually, we found a hotel (Hindustan International), not where we had reservations, and later discovered that the bottled water in the mini bar was faked.

Busy streets and traffic

Breakfast the next morning was a disaster, but we did manage to check out by 9.30 am. As usual, the first thing on our itinerary was some sightseeing, but Calcutta proved to be a little disappointing compared to Delhi.

We visited Indian Airlines and discussed business, but there was no enthusiasm.

Our next stop was Madras, and we were flying. One of our representatives called the airport and was told that we had standby seats 283 and 284. Not to be discouraged, we appeared at the check-in counter to be told by a supervisor that we were wasting our time asking – as we were already checked in! We had had seats the whole time as the tickets had been booked through Swissair – but it had caused some confusion. Further confusion had been caused by a plane change - 737 to an Airbus, and the flight had been rescheduled for 2.50 instead of 4.45 pm.

I must admit that I was looking forward to arriving and staying (hotel Taj Coromandel) for a few days in Madras. I had been living out of my suitcase since we arrived and now, I could finally empty my suitcase.

In Madras, we had several days of discussion with our agent (CUMI) and his representatives concerning potential and future business opportunities. It was mutually decided that we would spend the Sunday sightseeing. The idea was to drive south to visit the elephant monument (Mahabalipuram), a world heritage site. We were picked up in a car at 8.45 am, and before we had been driving for five minutes, the front seat collapsed. The solution was to drop us at an Indian outdoor restaurant for an Indian breakfast (our 2nd of the day) while the front seat was being welded back together! We drove about 55 km to the south, and the monument turned out to be very interesting. A collection of temples and shrines is located right beside the sea.

Visiting the Mahabalipuram temple

We weren't the only ones out for the day, and it was interesting to see many smiling, happy faces and the colourful clothes worn by the women.

Impressions from India

We had the opportunity to buy souvenirs after much haggling directly from the stone masons carving miniatures and enjoyed the local coconut juice.

We discovered that goats go crazy for the white coconut meat in the shell.

On the way back to Madras, we stopped at a beach hotel for lunch and bought souvenirs – seashells and, further up the coast, visited a crocodile farm that appeared to be full of crocodiles.

Visiting the crocodiles farm

We ended up walking along Marina Beach in Madras, getting back after dark to our hotel.

We were picked up on Monday morning and drove north to the CUMI office for about 20 minutes past fishermen's huts directly on the beach. Out on the water were catamarans and the typical boats with triangular sails. The morning and afternoon were filled with discussions and a visit to the local electricity board, but this was a waste of time. We had supper in the hotel coffee shop and left for the station taking the overnight train to Coimbatore, where a further customer event had been planned. We left from platform 9, and I was in berth 13. Despite the AC, it was a very hot and sticky night. Arriving at 6.25 am, we had no trouble finding a porter or a taxi, compared to other cities, and we made our way to our hotel (Hotel Surya International). The event started at 9.30 am and finished at 5.25 pm. We didn't seem to generate much interest.

For the next part of our journey, we took a car from Coimbatore to Cochin and then to Trivandrum to visit the Indian Space Centre. The drive at night was challenging for the driver as nothing on the road seemed to have lights. At one point, we almost collided with a cart pulled by two oxen- again with no lights.

It was very dark by the time we arrived in Cochin at 10.30 pm. We checked in (Abada Plaza) and went to our rooms for a quick clean-up before eating. Standing in the bathroom washing my face, I felt I wasn't alone. On my right, I detected movement, which turned out to be the largest cockroach I had ever seen. Having found one I started looking for more including stripping the bed and going over the curtains and I found a second large beastie crawling up the curtains. It didn't live for much longer, either.

The following day, we discovered that the hotel did not do breakfast, so we left early (7.20 am) and drove south to have breakfast in Alleppey (Alleppey Prince Hotel).

Along the coast through the Backwaters, we were surprised to see an amazing number of school children in uniform going to school. From the car, the views to the right towards the ocean were quite spectacular, with empty beaches and piers with fishing traps and further out fishing boats. On our way to Trivandrum, we even passed an elephant, trucks and carts loaded with straw, and several times we drove across sections of the road where the farmers had spread out their corn or rice, either to dry or be de-husked as we drove over it.

An elephant and a car all in the same lane

Bullock carts and heavy trucks

We finally arrived in Trivandrum at 1 pm at the hotel (Mascot Hotel, checked in, decided to go for an upgraded room and then headed off to the rocket centre, where we arrived late and got a good ticking-off. We had arranged 2 pm and arrived at 3.45 pm. We shortened our presentations which were not well received. Afterwards, we went to see Kovalam Beach but we didn't see very much as it was already dark. We had a drink at a local hotel and then found somewhere for dinner.

Street-side shops for food

At the hotel, I can recall asking for some washing done, and the shirts came back nicely washed, ironed, and wrapped individually in sheets of newspaper. Being so close to the southern tip of India, our driver asked if we wanted to go there to see the sun coming up. We declined, which was probably a big mistake. The following morning, we were expecting customers at our hotel for a meeting from 8 until 10 as we had a flight leaving at 11.55.

There was no hot water to shower, so the day had started well. Then we met for breakfast at 7, but it was served at 8, and then our customers finally arrived at 9.30.

We were booked to fly from Trivandrum to Bangalore and then to Madras. The flight to Bangalore was uneventful, but on boarding the plane for Madras we wondered what was dripping from the wings. As the pilot started the engines, the drip became a gush followed by a flood and the engine shut down. We had lost all the hydraulic fluid in the wing. On board was also a local state minister who had been driven out to the aircraft in a large Mercedes. We had to wait on board until his car had arrived to take him back to the departure lounge. We got off the plane and walked back to the waiting room.

The temperature on the tarmac was about 42°C, so we were glad to get inside where the air-con was running. Spare parts were available in Bombay and put on the next flight. After about 6 hours, we were ready to try again, and we finally reached Madras at 6.30 pm.

We stayed one day more in Madras for further discussions with our agent and his representatives and then, after lunch, flew to Bombay, where we had dinner and then on to the airport for an 11.30 departure to Zurich.

The plane had come in from Hongkong, and as we got on the plane, we saw the Swiss national football team with trainer Roy Hodgson re-boarding after training in Hongkong.

They were travelling in business class!

Kyoto, Osaka, Beijing, Zurich

July 1993

For whatever reason, I was in Osaka again. We must have been visiting Mitsubishi or even Tocalo. Anyway, the idea was that I would stay in Kyoto and spend the day with Mr. Oka from Tocalo. We got to know each other a little during his visits to Wohlen and his interest in VPS. We spent the day doing tourist things in Kyoto, a beautiful place with remarkable shrines. I spent the night at a hotel beside the station, knowing I could get the bus to Osaka airport from just across the street. Sometimes you get that funny feeling that earlier will be better than later, and I was at the stop with loads of time to waste.

However, when the bus arrived on time, I discovered two seats were available, and I was number 2 in line for the bus! I also discovered that Sunday was the start of a national holiday because the bus could only stop at the domestic terminal, about 500 metres from the international airport. Anyway, as a blob of sweat, from carrying my luggage, I checked in and found somewhere to wait. The plan was to fly from Osaka to Beijing with JAL and then to Zurich with Swissair. We got on the plane, and I discovered that the person on the inside seat had brought so much hand luggage that she could hardly move.

It was a lovely day when we landed in Beijing. We deplaned and walked towards the arrival building. Having been to China previously and experienced visa issues, I had started to have my doubts on the plane about how things work when you are in transit. On the way to arrivals, I saw the Beijing station manager of JAL walking along with us and asked him how this would work. Obviously, the question was the wrong one. He immediately got the ground staff to keep my bag on the ground. The JAL plane was parked right next to the Swissair plane, so my bags were simply moved from one to underneath the other. Then he started speaking rather hectically with somebody in arrivals on his two-way radio. At the building, he told me to follow him closely. We went in, and we headed for the crew entrance. My passport was reviewed and taken, and we proceeded up some stairs to the departure level, where I was led into departures and given back my passport. The guy had done a fantastic job, as I later realized. For transit/visa reasons, Swissair should never have issued a ticket with a transit stop in China!

Anyway, I thought, now I was on my way home! But of course, I still had to go to the Swissair desk and check in. It turned out that I was the last passenger to check in (!), and I got told off for being late!

Now armed with my boarding pass, I could proceed to the gate, get on the bus and finally get on the plane. At the gate, I waited surrounded by other passengers and as it happens I get the feeling that something is not right. You start to look around, see other people's tickets and decide that either they are wrong, you have missed your bus or the gate number is wrong. True to fame I go and ask and discover that the gate is for passengers going to Tokyo. It was for Zurich, but those passengers have left already! All is not lost, and I get a completely empty bus just for myself.

So now I was back on a Swissair MD11, sitting on a window seat on the right looking forward in economy knowing that we have about 10 hours to fly. What I came to appreciate was the clear visibility all the way across China and then Russia with the unending forests and especially the view of St. Petersburg from over 10000 metres of altitude.

The person on the aisle seat was an Austrian service engineer sent to China originally for 6 weeks and now after 3 months, he is able to fly home.

We really did enjoy the bottle of red wine which was smuggled out of business class for us!

Tokyo to Singapore

November 1993

What do you do on a Saturday on a long trip?

Finding yourself alone in Tokyo and not knowing what to do or how to do it, you continue to travel. I had agreed to run a thermal spray one-day meeting with Bob Clarke in Singapore. I have lined up to take the 12 o'clock flight to Singapore on a Singapore Airlines flight in economy. The plane is a 747, and I have an aisle seat beside the door close to the toilet block. The plane had started in Osaka, so it was already quite full when it arrived in Tokyo. We were in the air, having been fed, when a short, old-aged person struggled down the aisle towards me. I noticed it wasn't much of a struggle but more like the tango of a Japanese male who had already consumed too much alcohol. He turned to his left and disappeared into the bathroom.

By this time, most people were asleep, so when he came back out, did a double pirouette, and fell, sledgehammer-like, onto his back and started to vomit, there weren't many awake to see it happen.

Like any boy scout, I got up and turned his head to the side - just so that he wouldn't die of suffocation. I suppose I must have been a little on the loud side because soon, I was surrounded by many flight attendants who imagined that I had attacked the guy and knocked him down. The senior flight attendant gave me a real mouthful about behaviour in flight, and luckily at least the vomit changed their opinion. It was cleared up very quickly, and the area was sprayed so that there was no more odour.

The guy even got changed sometime later and came to thank me for helping him, in fact he came past every time he went to the bathroom. I just returned to my seat and tried to relax after hearing all the negative comments from the flight attendants. We were just three hours into a 7 to 8-hour flight, and I was not happy on reflection. In the meantime, the senior flight attendant had rethought his position and approached me rather timidly, asking if he could get me anything.

I decided that I would like a Japanese beer. In fact, it turned out to be many beers because every time the glass got half empty, somebody popped by and refilled it. This went well - for a Saturday afternoon, but it did not help me very much on leaving the plane and entering Changi airport with an outside temperature over 30°C.

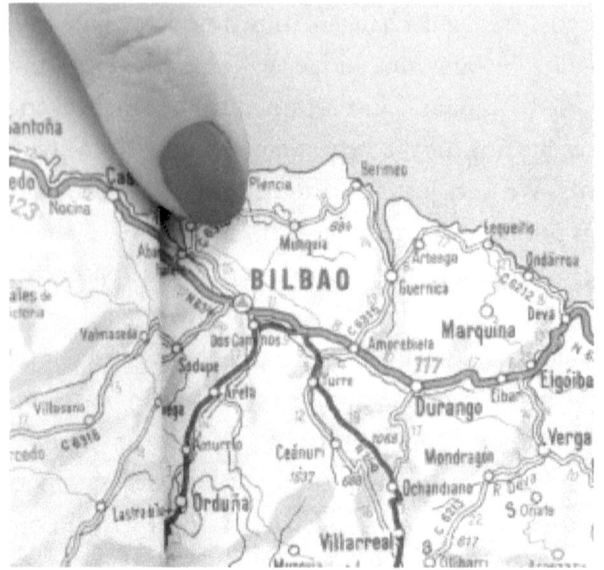
Santoña
edo
Cab
Bermeo
Nocina
Plencia
Munguia
Lequeitio
Abas
Arteaga
Ondárroa
BILBAO
Guernica
ales de
Deva
ctoria
Marquina
Valmaseda
Dos Caminos
Amorebieta
Villasano
Sadupe
777
Areta
urre
Elgóibar
Eibar
Durango
vega
Verga
Ceánuri
Amurrio
Mondragón
Orduña
Ochandiano
S. Oñate
Lastra
Villarreal

Bilbao & San Sebastian

Spain

1994

San Sebastian is such a nice place, but why do things seem to go wrong when I am there? They have an excellent regional institute that puts on meetings, and I am here to speak about Surface Engineering. Friendly crowd and no lousy questions. Lovely old town nice tapas in fact, a really nice place.

We spent the next morning at the institute exploring possible areas for joint projects, and then it was time to head back to the airport in Bilbao. After about 30 minutes on the highway, I sort of get this inkling that something is not right, and our salesman in Spain decides that he is driving in the wrong direction. We turn around and head back in the other direction. By now, of course, the time has been lost, and the plane won't wait.

I arrived at the airport 10 minutes before the departure time and had a problem convincing the Swissair ground crew that I was really getting on that plane, standing just 25 metres outside the building. By chance, somebody from the plane comes and asks if I might be the last passenger.

Ah, the joys of flying!

Tokyo

Company Integration

1994

Setting up a company and doing business locally in a completely different culture to your own takes time and patience. We formed a company with Marubeni in Japan to look after our surface engineering interests. We found that we could work well with them, but as time progressed, we had to recognize that we were only doing business with companies close to or directly associated with Marubeni. This meant that we were missing out on market opportunities.

We decided that it was time to split. As with all changes in Japan, it had to be celebrated by an evening event in a Tokyo hotel with all of our customers being formally invited. There were speeches, food, and toasting of the new company's success.

Cultures can be different, but this took me back a bit. Looking around the room, I saw that we had done well in attracting many customers but that it was a strictly male event. Not even our own back-office ladies were in attendance. After the event, I asked if this was normal, and I got that look in reply, which said I shouldn't be asking the question.

Later in the merger with Metco to form Sulzer Metco in Japan that same thing occurred – but I had learned my lesson the first time.

Zurich, Stockholm, London, LA, Cincinnati, Chicago, Zurich

September 1994

As Chairman of the ASM European Council, I volunteered to give a brief welcoming speech at an ASM conference in Stockholm and then leave again. It wasn't a conference where I could stay, listen, and gain information. It was all well above my head.

It was the day that the ferry Estonia went down (28th September 1994), and the emotions across Sweden were running high.

I needed to be at our facility in Los Angeles for an internal product seminar directly after the event in Stockholm. It turned out that I could fly to Stockholm the night before, give my speech the following morning and get to the airport in time for the flight to London connecting onwards to LA. Funnily, the ticket to LA from Zürich was the same price as my roundabout trip through Stockholm, London, and LA.

I was at the window with two pilots from SAS sitting next to me going to London to find their planes (as if they had lost them!). It turned out that they were flying the same type of plane, a DC9, with mechanical controls, and they spent some time explaining how it all worked – mechanically speaking.

At Heathrow, I found Terminal 4 and eventually boarded. I was sitting on the aisle with somebody from Finland at the window. He had already drunk too much. I wondered how he even managed to be allowed on the plane. There must be something about the Finns outside of Finland and alcohol. LA is an 11 to 12-hour flight from London, and he slept quite well. I was picked up by one of my colleagues at the airport, and we went to join all the other members of the seminar group for dinner. It was quite a temperature shock, having started early in Stockholm and then sitting outside having dinner in LA experiencing earth tremors.

The plan to get back to Europe was to fly to Cincinnati to visit GEAE, then to Chicago and back to Zürich. This would have been OK, except that we had a 5-hour delay in LA as the rudder on the plane was not operating correctly. This put us into an early morning arrival in Cincinnati, we couldn't find the car in long term parking and, consequently, a poorly prepared meeting at GEAE.

Sometimes bad things just happen.

Bilbao

Spain

1994

The call from Swissair was a surprise. The Iberia flight is cancelled. Can I fly on the Swissair flight, which is an hour earlier?

OK, no big deal and costs the same and is going to the same place – Barcelona with a continuing flight to Bilbao.

But what we wanted to do was get to San Sebastian.

The chaos started on arriving in Barcelona. There were Iberia people trying to get me off one plane and onto another, but then in the middle of it all, I met up with our salesperson and our local agent. All flights are cancelled so we have to hire a car. We drove to San Sebastian arriving in time for dinner, i.e. Spanish style, after 10 pm.

Whatever we did on the next day I don't recall anymore, but I do know that I was handed the car keys in the afternoon, and it was suggested that I could get home by driving the car over the border to Biarritz airport, taking the shuttle flight to Paris, taking the bus to Charles de Gaulle airport and the last flight to Zurich.

Which is what I did!

Tokyo

Japan

May 1995

In every organization, there are people who just meet after work and enjoy a drink. In Japan, it seems to be more of the older crowd drinking sake. It turns out that our controller in Japan spent all his time at university, testing sake, until he became an expert.

During one of these sessions, he asked me if I played tennis. Without thinking about it, I replied yes, I do, and so it became clear:

"The next time you are in Japan, we will play tennis together."

In May 1995, we had an exhibition and conference in Kobe, a city partly destroyed by an earthquake. From my hotel room, I looked down at an overhead motorway that had completely collapsed. I had packed my tennis kit and racket and explained that I could come up to Tokyo on a Friday evening and we could get together on Saturday.

"What colour do you normally wear?"

"Anything that fits, in Europe, it's not so much a question of colour."

"Here at the club (Japan Lawn Tennis Association), we have to wear white, so I will pick you up at the station, and then we will go shopping."

Serious stuff!

Luckily, he knew which store stocked the super sizes, and for a small fortune, I was kitted out.

The following day, we met at the hotel and made our way in a taxi to the tennis club, where I was admitted for the day as a guest. We got changed – into our whites and joined the other members on the terrace. After introductions, we made up a four and went off to play. The clay courts were laid out in a line directly in front of the terrace, so many people were watching and offering comments.

The members were professionals who had worked in Europe or the USA and spoke English well. It seemed to me that we played nonstop for hours. Every time we finished a set, there were new partners and off we went again, in addition to a small or even a large beer in between.

It was a hot day, and after about 6 hours, we were suffering, so we started to slow down and spend more time on the terrace. By now, several members were suffering from the alcohol and hot weather.

There had been little food all day, so eventually, we got around to the question of dinner, showered, changed, and left.

It turned out that the members thought that I played quite nicely, even if a little old-fashioned - so I could come again if I wanted!

Sunds in Sundsvall
Sweden

November 1996

I had flown to Stockholm, met one of our salespeople at the airport, and we had driven for 4 hours to Sunds in the north of Sweden.

It was cold and unexciting all the way to Sunds with very few cars and nothing to see; it was already dark. We stayed at a local Scandic hotel and the following day went to Sundsvall to meet our customer. Driving into the car park, I was interested in what the posts were for in front of every parking spot. When the driver got out, went to the front of the Volvo, pulled out an electric cable, and plugged it in, I realized that the car had oil sump heating. Mind you, it was minus 14°C.

The person we were visiting had just joined the company and wanted to install new equipment and use consumables from our competition. He wanted to have our presentation and the following discussion in the Swedish language. After having come so far, it was rather depressing to hear that, especially as we knew he spoke excellent English. Before going to lunch, we had a tour of the workshop, which did not give the impression that they had enough business. Over lunch, the opportunity occurred that I could ask a few questions in English, and it seemed, with the technical discussion and the answers we provided, that the ice had been broken, and the afternoon proceeded far more positively, with everybody appearing happy.

View from the hotel (sketch by the author)

The following day, we left, and we drove back towards Stockholm. I had a taxi ordered to get me to the airport for the first plane to Zurich. I was dropped off at a Scandic hotel in Uppsala. It was still light but getting dark quickly as we arrived, and after a couple of hours, it became cold.

Katowice
Poland

November 1996

We were a party of three flying to Katowice from Frankfurt and were met at the airport. It was very dark when we reached the hotel, and everything was poorly lit compared to Frankfurt.

The hotel had been built in the typical "Eastern Block" style, the kind of hotel you find in all the communist countries.

Looking out of the window of my hotel room the following day, I saw that we were right next to a coal mine on one side and on the other, what seemed to be apartment buildings and a sports arena.

It was all rather dark from coal dust.

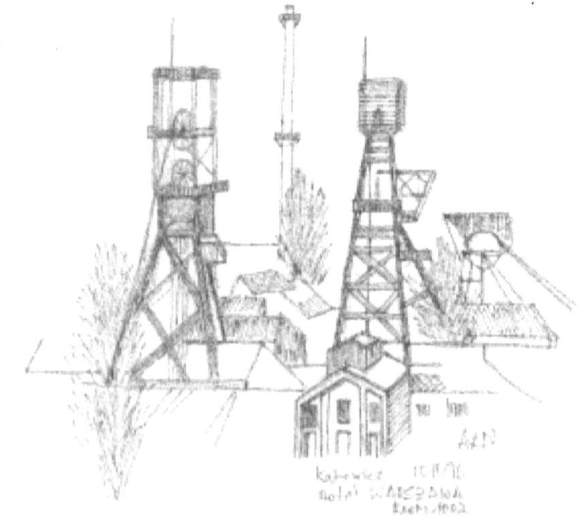

View from the hotel (author's sketches)

Singapore, Hong Kong, San Francisco, Cincinnati

1996

I was in Singapore for a company event and had to get to a conference (NTSC) in Cincinnati.

"Not a problem, sir. We can book you through".

I think I was flying with United Airlines, and we started early in the morning in Singapore. The plane was nearly empty, and I had a window seat, which on this trip is great for watching the ocean, but on the other hand, there is nothing else to see. We had breakfast, and after 3 hours, we descended into Hongkong, the old airport where we were asked to leave the plane as transit passengers. We had about an hour to wait before the next departure, and after 30 minutes, we were asked to go back on board, much to the disgust of quite a few passengers who had been waiting quite a while and thought they should have priority. After we were seated, they were allowed on, giving us filthy looks.

We left, and soon the lunch service started. What I can remember next is that I woke up as we were on our approach to San Francisco, and I had slept from the end of lunch across the Pacific, missed breakfast, and here we were entering the States.

For whatever reason, my business class seat across the Pacific put me into first class on the flight to Cincinnati, so I was offered drinks and fed again.

By the time I had recovered my bags, taken a taxi from the airport to the conference hotel, checked in, and found my room, I was in a bit of a daze, to say the least. Luckily it was still Saturday, so at least I still had Sunday to regain some sanity.

Sao Paulo
Brazil

August 1997

As the marketing specialist for automotive applications, I was going to Brazil for a week, taking the late Friday night plane directly from Zurich to Sao Paulo.

The waiting area in Zurich was filled with Brazilian style music as we waited to board, coming from students returning to Brazil with their boom machines.

Just to be sure about the weather, I had called our people in Brazil before leaving the office and asked what it was like and discovered that the temperature was a high 20-23° and improving. My conclusion was that I wouldn't need a coat, so I left for Brazil in a sweater.

At about 6 am the next morning approaching the airport, we were woken by the pilot who calmly announced that the outside temperature in Sao Paulo was 9°! I spent the weekend feeling the cold.

Together with our Brazilian representatives, we visited Mercedes, VW, Volvo, and ZF, either in Sao Paulo or Curitiba, and various local job shops supplying the auto industry. Many of the people we met at these companies came originally from Germany or Sweden.

Flying was interesting as it meant flying over areas with no roads, just jungle.

Whatever we did, we couldn't avoid the music or the football. In the hotels and restaurants, there was either music that made you want to move to the music, or they were replaying all the football matches from the previous weekend.

On Saturday night, all of us were invited to a large restaurant/music hall, large enough to cover a football pitch easily. You entered in the middle, and families sat at long tables on one side, and singles sat on the other side. Food and wine just kept coming, and the live music was very good.

At the airport on Friday afternoon, I went into the duty-free shop and bought my wife a present using a credit card. I had seat 14F and was one of the very few getting on the plane in Sao Paulo, in fact, most passengers were coming from Rio. I got on, took my seat, and got comfortable. It was then that I noticed a woman hovering near my seat. She kept looking backwards and forwards, and then she disappeared towards the front door and started speaking with a flight attendant.

I thought nothing about it until a nice-looking female purser came to my seat, crouched down and asked me very quietly to gather my things and follow her forward. Seat 14F became 1B, and I was very happy for the next 10 hours, including the visit to the cockpit. Shortly afterwards, back in Switzerland, the credit card company called me and informed me that my card was being replaced - I had used the card twice, once to pay for the hotel and once at the duty-free shop in Sao Paulo!

Atlanta

USA

April 1998

Transit desks can be dangerous, especially if your wife travels with you.

We arrived at the transit desk in Atlanta between Orlando and Zurich. I approached the desk about boarding cards for the Swissair connection, and my wife chirped in, asking about an upgrade.

"Well, let's see, sir, you have over 600'000 miles in your account."

To which my wife responded - "You have how many?"

As luck would have it, my wife was already flying on an upgraded ticket, so a further upgrade didn't happen.

But now she knew how many miles I had in my account with Swissair!

I had two gin & tonics on the plane and snored all the way to Zurich.

Montreal
Canada

January 1998

Since 5th January, we have seen television reports of the damage occurring in Canada due to the freezing rain and hailstones. And to cap it all, we have a Pulp & Paper exhibition in Montreal, and I have been asked to attend as the Marketing Specialist. Zurich to Montreal with Swissair is easy, comfortable, and convenient. It was getting dark already as we arrived. The taxi to the hotel was cold and drafty. The Sheraton hotel was not much better, and after a quick supper and a drink, it was off to bed. The following day, I discovered that the temperature outside had been 18°C below zero.

The positive thing about the cold weather is that the view from my window across the city was superb. Looking down from my room window, I recognised the Montreal cathedral and saw that the trees surrounding the square had lost most of their branches due to the weight of the freezing rain.

With temperatures so low outside, Montreal has at least the luxury of underground walkways connecting most buildings in the city's centre.

Montreal, Canada

Therefore, getting to the congress centre was easy without exposure to the outside temperatures and the wind. The exhibition was held in the congress centre I visited in 1986 for the ITSC.

Malaga Granada
Spain

1998

I was asked by the head of sales for Europe (Jordi Garcia) to organize a small exhibition booth at a powder conference in Granada. I was in the Global Marketing group responsible for Europe, and the political twist was that several of Jordi's Spanish friends were involved in organizing the conference, and they needed more exhibitors. This Powder Conference is global and only takes place every three years. Looking at the conference program, we shouldn't have been there at all.

In the conference program, there was a special bus connection arranged from Malaga airport to Granada. The bus had already left before my flight arrived, so I took a rental car and drove to Granada, mostly passing through orange plantations. With some time available, I took the opportunity to visit the cathedral, which definitely has to be one of the most peculiar designs I have ever seen. Jordi and the head of sales for Spain participated and we also had dinner together although they didn't think the food for Spain was so good. We had a small booth, 3m x 3m, at the exhibition, sufficient for some posters, a small table for brochures, and a chair. The following night I had dinner with a salesperson from the Spanish office, and we found a nice old restaurant in the old part of the city, which turned out to be excellent.

The following evening, I was given an invitation from Jordi to attend an evening dinner sponsored by Högenäs (a large powder producing company) held in a bullfighting ring. We had buses from the hotel and back again afterwards, which was very advantageous because of the quantities of alcohol which had been consumed, mostly Scandinavian schnapps. Breakfast with Jordi the next morning was not a happy event. He had given me the invitation because he wanted to leave early and needed to be fit, and I had enjoyed myself sufficiently that I needed to stay in bed.

The conference was of no interest to me, and the booth was being looked after by the Spanish salesperson, so I had time to visit the Alhambra, which was located just a short walk up the road from the hotel. It was my first experience buying an entrance ticket with time limitations for certain parts of Alhambra. Superb architecture and, interestingly, some parts with the same interior ceiling design as I had seen in the Red Fort in Delhi, India. Afterwards, I discovered that it was the Moors (Muslim Arabs) from the North African coast who had invaded Spain in the 8th century and the Muslim Arabs who had invaded India from the north, thus resulting in the same architectural direction and interior design. Before leaving the Alhambra, I bought a small box as a souvenir in Spanish style at the gift shop on the way out. The salesperson thought I was a visitor from Brazil!

Plzen (Pilsen)
Czech Republic

1999

When the word Plzen is heard, one immediately thinks about beer. In fact, we discovered that there are really three different breweries in the town. We had spent the morning in Prague visiting the castle and then made our way to Plzen where I had to give a short welcoming speech for the ASM at a conference. On the way, I discovered that the driver uses the tram to get to work on a daily basis and sometimes, at the weekend, gets to use the car. Here he was, now in a company car driving to Plzen. We got there without incident, found the university and then the hotel, and then the beer.

The following day, we drove back to the airport in Prague. My driver was now a lot more confident and decided to take a shorter scenic route back to the airport through the countryside. Fabulous countryside and curving roads, but instead of keeping our speed up, we had to stop for unmanned rail crossings. By the 3rd one, I was becoming impatient and urging the driver to keep going. We could see across the fields, and no trains were in sight. At the next one, the driver stopped anyway, and from nowhere, a train appeared at speed and flashed through.

It was very quiet in the car back to the airport.

Hartford

USA

2001

As a Trustee (i.e., member of the board) of the ASM International, I was obliged to attend meetings in Cleveland or other wonderful places in the US rust belt every 3-4 months.

There was also an expectation that Trustees would feel the pulse of their members by attending local chapter meetings and sometimes giving short talks. So I was in Hartford, having arrived from Cleveland to give a talk on Surface Engineering to the local chapter.

The talk was fine, the attendance low, and we found ourselves in a live music bar close to the hotel after dinner. I arranged a late check-out the following day as I had a 2 pm flight to Kennedy connecting to the Swissair flight at 6.30 pm to Zurich.

And then it started to snow!

Watching large snowflakes descend slowly can be very relaxing, except when you start worrying about your connecting flight and the alternative.

"Yes, sir, there is a limo bus leaving Hartford at 12 today going non-stop to Kennedy".

"OK, I will think about it".

The snow got heavier and heavier and started to pile up nicely on the street. I decided to head for the airport – fast. I arrived at Hartford airport and checked in with American Airlines. After about 5 minutes of searching for a seat, an announcement was made that the flight to Kennedy was cancelled as the propeller machine would not be able to get above the snow level in the clouds. I took my briefcase and coat and went through into the departure area and then realized that it was jammed packed, i.e., no planes were departing.

I returned to the front desk and asked what the deal was. Next to me, another person was going to Kennedy, and he was offered a taxi ride to Kennedy. I managed to get my luggage back and ride with him to Kennedy. We drove for about 15 minutes on the highway from Hartford, and the snow stopped. The taxi turned out to be a large Chevrolet Estate, and yes, his friend had fixed the engine, suspension, and brakes so that we could chug along quite nicely, thank you very much.

We got to the Swissair terminal building at 6.10 pm, and I could check in but had to carry my luggage to the plane myself.

I made it to the gate by 6.25 pm.

Cleveland

USA

Without power

2003

I am travelling to Cleveland for an ASM board meeting.

As I got onto the hotel shuttle bus at Cleveland airport, all the lights in the airport, in all the buildings and the hotel went out. Although the hotel can be seen from the arrival building, you can't walk to the hotel, vehicles only.

Not that you would usually notice that the lights had gone out, but as we approached the hotel car park, the barrier would not go up, and it was then that we started to recognize that the electric power was gone.

Checking in at the hotel was impossible – no computers were running, and "Please would you come back later".

Our meeting was supposed to be in one of the meeting rooms in the basement, a room without windows, so we took over the bar and positioned some tables next to the windows. That's where we stayed for the next 6 hours, having our meeting and enjoying whatever food they had available.

Sometime in the afternoon, we tried to check in again, and this time we were given room numbers and keys. After dinner, we were each given a couple of candles and a box of matches. During the night my door handle was tried several times, I suppose people trying to find somewhere to sleep. I left a light switched on so I could check when the power returned.

The next morning, we had power, the telephones worked, and everybody got back to normal, and the hotel didn't charge me for the room because of the inconvenience.

It turned out that the area south of Cleveland had not been affected at all. The major power outage had hit everybody to the north into Canada and east across to Long Island where we were living at the time.

New York to Zürich
Flying Yellow

2004

Sketching in transit

So, you got an upgrade to first class on Swissair to Zurich, so what's the fuss about?

"Well," I said a little shy, "it's a little difficult to explain because it was yellow."

"Yellow?"

"Yes, yellow!"

"Yellow door select to automatic," the captain said, and we were off, number 12 in the line for take-off—a typical Friday night at Kennedy Airport.

Newspapers were read and dumped on the empty seat next to me. We got to altitude, and the dinner service began with drinks and a white tablecloth with some nice silver and salt and pepper and then – a yellow rose. A small, closed yellow rose, closed up for protection, I thought but with nowhere to stand.

The surprising thing about the gap between two aeroplane seats is that there is nowhere for a rose stem to stand for the length of the flight without any help. I mean, if you are in seat 2A and you want to enjoy the colour of the neighbourhood, then the head of a rose definitely needs elevation. In this case, the rose only got my genuine appreciation as my head slowly sank after the meal and into the night.

Sometime later they faded the lights so that we could try to sleep, and the colour lost its significance. Sometime in the night, it decided to leave me. I must have turned over and knocked it from its position.

If it had been my wife, she would have hit me back.

Now that's colour.

Dayton
USA

2006

It was a Thursday afternoon, and the phone rang. "Can you be in Dayton for a meeting on Tuesday morning?"

A quick look at my calendar in Outlook told me that I was free, and a call to the travel office got me booked from Zurich to Chicago and onto Dayton and back again. An e-mail arrived during the afternoon confirming my hotel reservation in the centre of town, so I was ready to go; everything was fine – except that I didn't have much clue about the problem or where Dayton was located.

The problem was not fixed quickly, and I returned to Dayton several times before we became confident in what we were doing.

On one trip, I was taken to the Engineers Club in Dayton by Terry Nels for lunch. Founded in 1914, it is a building with a lot of polished dark wood, and of course, I had to have the tour. One of the main exhibits is a mechanical cash register, and I learnt very quickly that Dayton was the home of NCR (National Cash Registers). At the club, engineers from all walks of life would meet monthly. The NCR engineers got together with a company making generators to charge batteries for cars, and electric motors were designed and tested, leading to the electric cash register. The electrical company was Delco. Terry Nels had been to Germany several times to collect a VW bus, take a vacation and then ship the vehicle back to the USA.

It turned out that his favourite spot in Switzerland had always been Andermatt. As we had always visited Andermatt both in winter and summer, I was able to provide him with a CD of all my photos.

I always stayed at the Crowne Plaza Hotel in the middle of town. Almost opposite on North Main Str. is a sculpture – "The Flyover" – to track the path of the Wright brother's first powered aeroplane flight.

In 2002 my wife and I relocated to Long Island, NY and discovered the "Cradle of Aviation Museum" near the Marriott Hotel in Uniondale and the Nassau Coliseum, where the Islanders play ice hockey. The museum tracks the history of flight on Long Island, starting with the wealthy financiers having weekend houses on the north shore. Being bored, they decided flying would be interesting, so Mitchell Field was established with companies giving flying lessons. The airport eventually turned into the largest training centre in WWII for fighter pilots. Long Island, during WWII was also the manufacturing centre for fighter planes. The financiers also built a 71-mile racetrack which today forms part of the Northern State Parkway.

The museum also covers the history of the Wright brothers, who were at home in Dayton running a bicycle store but interested in the design of wings to get lift, i.e., go up and thus fly. They contacted the Meteorological Office at that time in Washington, DC, requesting information on a possible location with a certain wind speed where they could test their wing constructions. This turned out to be Kill Devil Hill on the Outer Banks near Kitty Hawk (today). In their time, the Outer Banks were only inhabited by fishermen in the summer.

So off they went from Dayton to the Outer Banks for several years running to do their testing with gliders until that famous day when they flew. During WWI, the brothers negotiated with the French on their plane designs and patents, but it didn't proceed very far. With one brother suddenly dying, the other brother didn't have any more interest in flying, and their work was taken over by Curtis, forming the Curtis-Wright company. We decided it would be interesting to visit the Outer Banks and the Wright Brothers Museum and Memorial at Kill Devil Hill and see the replica of the original plane they used. On the way there, we stopped in Williamsburg (the original capital of Virginia) and came across an exhibition of old maps, including what was to become New York. It showed Manhattan and Long Island, both being described as summer pastures and across Manhattan were two tracks, one north–south and the other east-west.

Time has moved on.

P.S. Lunch at the club was the day's special – cheeseburger with double bacon, fries on the side and a coke. It was perfect!

TRAVEL ANECDOTES
ANDREW R. NICOLL
BUSINESS

Epilogue

2009

In 2009 I had an operation planned at the end of March—a stomach bypass operation to help me lose weight.

However, on the 19th of February, we had a company information meeting in one of the equipment halls, and management informed us that we would be losing people.

An hour later, the telephone rang, and I was requested to go to the HR office. Immediately the idea flashed through my mind that my name was on the list. In the office, I was informed that due to financial issues, personnel were being let go, including me. It took 10 minutes; I returned to my office and later went home. After 26 years, it was a shock.

Something went wrong with the operation, and it took until January 2010 before I was medically fit to work again. I was registered as unemployed for nearly two years, but during this time, something interesting happened. I started to get calls from companies that I had visited who now needed help, even from the competition. I set up a website and started to get inquiries which led me to company visits in Germany, Ireland, France, Canada, and the USA.

In 2019, I had a project with a medical company in Switzerland, and the European management had approved an investment of over €8 Mio. However, the project also had to be approved by management in the USA, and, at the time, President Trump had stated that US companies should invest in the USA (make America great again). So, the project was dropped— and I finally retired!

Glossary
Thermal Spray

"Is a coating deposition process in which a consumable in the form of wire or powder is introduced into a heat source, gas or electric, becomes heated or even molten, and is accelerated by hot or cold gas towards the surface to be coated. By moving the heat source relative to the surface, the coating is built up to the required thickness."

ASM: American Society of Materials
ITSC: International Thermal Spray Conference
NTSC: National Thermal Spray Conference
OEM: Original Equipment Manufacturers
BAMTRI: Original representative of Plasma Technik in China
CUMI: Original representative of Plasma Technik in India
Ravi, Kamban; Sales employees of CUMI
Erich Brenner: Sales Director (Asia, Soviet Union, PRC)
Dieter Schmid: Sales India
C.T.Tan; Sales Singapore & PRC
Terry Nels: Lead engineer at Sulzer Euroflamm in Dayton, Ohio, U.S.A.
Jordi Garcia; Sales Spain, Portugal - then European Sales Director
VPS: Vacuum Plasma Spray
UPS: Underwater Plasma Spraying
HAECO: In Hongkong; servicing Cathy Pacific planes with Rolls Royce engines
Marubeni: Large trading house in Japan
Mr. Oka; Head of R&D at Tocalo
Mr. Nakahira; President of Tocalo

About the Author

Andrew R. Nicoll

C.Eng., FASM; FIMMM; ASM-HoF

Andrew R. Nicoll was born in Exeter, Devon, England, in 1949, attended Hele's Grammar School, Exeter, and studied Metallurgy and Materials Technology at the University of Surrey in Guildford, Surrey. This was followed in 1971 by unemployment and then an opportunity to work for Brown Boveri in Baden, Switzerland. He moved to Germany in 1973, returning to Plasma Technik AG in Switzerland in 1984. He accompanied the global growth of this company and its merger with Metco in 1994, forming Sulzer Metco, a leading player in Surface Engineering. He has worked in many different positions both in Europe and the USA as well as supporting Sulzer Metco companies located around the world. In addition, he played an active role in the American Society of Materials International, especially in conference planning, being nominated for president in 2004. Unfortunately, he had to step down for medical reasons.

On 20th February 2009, his position was eliminated because of the "economic crisis". This was followed by planned surgery which unfortunately became complicated, keeping him out of action for six months. After returning to good health, he found sufficient demand as a consultant in Europe, the USA, and Canada to continue until 2019, when he finally retired.

Now with plenty of time on his hands, he was able to review his travels over the last 25 years. Having kept his boarding cards from over 900 flights, he could reconstruct many of his business trips and the incidents that happened along the way. Together with photographs taken and sketches made during many trips, this book tries to capture the spirit of the past in short story form.

BOSE CREATIVE PUBLISHERS

www.bosecreativepublishers.ch

Bose Creative Publishers (BCP), established in 2020 in Switzerland, is a collaborative publishing company which promotes 'creative activism' and encourages creativity in everyday life to bring about a social change or create a positive impact. Book sales profit fund NGOs working for the underprivileged around the world. BCP's writers, contributors, and editors work as volunteers. Books Published include the following:

1. Sketching Diaries, 2020
2. Social Entrepreneurs and Change Makers, 2020
3. She Reflects, 2021
4. Indian Grandmas Secret Recipes, 2021
5. Emotions in Rhythm, 2021
6. She Celebrates, 2021
7. In Search of Sherpur: An Immigrant's Memoir, 2021
8. She Shines, 2022
9. Wanderlust – Travel Stories, 2022
10. She Seeks, 2023
11. Business Travel Anecdotes, 2023

www.bosecreativepublishers.ch[1]

bosecreativepublishers@gmail.com
All books are available at major online portals.

1. http://www.bosecreativepublishers.ch

15 travellers have come together to write this book of anecdotes and essays from their recent travels around the world. From ship voyages to fishing in Alaska to visiting India's ancient forts and walls, to reaching the ends of the world in both poles. This book is unique when you read the stories shared across Alaska, Argentina, Armenia, Italy, France, India, Mexico, South Africa, Turkey, and Indonesia. Grab a copy of the book.

Seven global social entrepreneurs (founders and leaders) share their advice. This book features seven founders of social enterprises from India, Switzerland, South Africa and the US. With case studies and interviews, this book talks about how and why these leaders started their social projects and how we, as a community, can support such causes. It talks about projects to support textiles from conflict zones, educate the underprivileged, or empower women with handicrafts and skills. Each social entrepreneur adds his or her personal note, which makes the book very interesting to read.

Authentic recipes from 16 Indian grandmas and their families. Published in 2021. This book features 25 authentic regional delicacies from 16 Indian grandmas across India. conceptualised by Mrs. Debjani Dutta (a grandma herself), this book includes recipes from grandmas who are 70 to 95 years old from various parts of India. It also has legacy recipes passed on by family members. During the pandemic it took almost two years for the collaborators to put together this book.

This book has 43 flash fictions. Written by 22 women, it follows the journey of river Ganga, with female protagonists experiencing different stages of life, in 43 micro stories. The book starts with a story set in Kilimanjaro, and ends with a story in the mother's womb.

This book is a memoir written by Prof. J. Bhattacharyya, US; and his search for home, describing his journey from early childhood when he had to leave his home in Sherpur, as an immigrant travel to Kolkata during the partition. Then he went to Delhi, later travelled to Brussels and settled down in the US. With stand-alone chapters which are hilarious as well as stories lined with pain of separation from home, family and friends. Expats and immigrants will connect with this book immediately.

Five Swiss artists share their urbansketches and paintings from around the world, and from Switzerland. Paintings are done from hotel rooms in Australia, to skyline sketches from New York, this book takes you round the world with anecdotes and sketching tips, and encourages all to pick up a paper and pencil, and indulge in a drawing experience. This book is in colour and has two sections (world travels and Switzerland).

The stories in 'She Shines' are like myriad precious stones in a necklace, strung together through a common thread, yet each stone has a shape and colour of its own. This common thread is resilience. The female gender throughout cultures, and perhaps through her own unique feminine stance, has borne the brunt of many impossible circumstances. Yet, within her, certain persistence and forbearance exist, that can turn things around. Stories of resilience and victory, are seasoned with two different flavours - the real and the surreal.

This book has 21 short stories, based on 21 Indian festivals, showcasing India's rich cultural heritage. Wherever we live in the world, we keep these traditions close to our heart. Each story ends with a festive recipe and an illustration, festivals include Lohri, to Eid; Durga Puja to Christmas, and many exotic festivals from all parts of India. This book also has small festive drawings by the authors after each story.

A Collection of poems by women of Indian origin, this book explores a potpourri of emotions. Our poets talk about fleeting moments, impressions, and their perceptions, in poems. Written by women coming from different professional backgrounds, this book is a delight to read, and gift to poetry lovers.

The stories in She Seeks essentially revolve around how humans have used their minds to navigate a complex world. The mind, in constant interaction with a dynamic environment, is perpetually seeking answers. Sometimes this takes the form of a yearning for or a desire to connect with the past—often termed as nostalgia. The journey down the memory lane can shed a light on a present predicament or a problem or lead to new self-realizations.

Thank you for buying this book, hope you enjoyed reading it. Make sure you have the other books in your personal collection too!

www.ingramcontent.com/pod-product-compliance
Lightning Source LLC
La Vergne TN
LVHW091253190726
843491LV00001B/250